Anatomy of a Tear

Anatomy of a Tear

A Chaplain's Stories of Life, Love & Loss

Chaplain Leon H. Olenick, BCC

Soul Geology Books

Boulder, Colorado

2013

Life affirming true stories of a Chaplain's encounters with patients, their families and caregivers as he witnesses their tears of joy and heartache during life's most profound moments.

Soul Geology Books
P.O. Box 19682
Boulder, CO 80308
www.geologistsofthesoul.com
publisher@soulgeologybooks.com

Edited and prepared for publication by Amitai Zachary Malone.

Cover artwork by Jackie Olenick.

Patient–Chaplain interactions are both highly personal and confidential. Professional chaplains are seldom called upon except at the most sensitive and oftentimes gut-wrenching moments in a person's life. Patients and their families must feel a complete sense of privacy and know that their communications are protected, which they are. All the stories in this manuscript are factual but names have been changed and sometimes events altered slightly.

Manufactured in the United States of America

ISBN-13: 978-0615911106
ISBN-10: 0615911102

Advance Praise for *Anatomy of a Tear*

"Such a blessing for us! Leon Olenick gives us stories so simply profound they touch all the organs of the body, tenderizing the heart, assisting the liver to live a life worth living! More than that, they render the soul so it might emerge clarified. This is an enduring and precious read."

Mitchell Chefitz, author of
The Seventh Telling and *The Curse of Blessings*

"These magnificent stories are filled with insightful, creative, and often replicable acts of compassion and loving-kindness direly needed in healthcare settings today. This master chaplain reveals how to extend the beauty and meaning of living into every last moment."

Rabbi Goldie Milgram, author of
Mitzvah Stories: Seeds for Inspiration and Learning

"My eyes mist as I enter these sacred encounters. These moments become unforgettable and now live within me. I am forever grateful to Leon for remembering these times and for sharing their majesty. I find my spirit renewed as I recognize myself "living in black and white rather than Technicolor." The images drawn from these relationships will give new meaning to all who draw near. May the sweet water of the tears herein flow through you and renew."

Martha Rutland, ACPE Supervisor,
Board Certified Chaplain, United Methodist Minister

"Leon Olenick managed to integrate all the required learning to be a Rabbi and chaplain with the heart. This book is a heart opener for clergy and their work and for people who seek out clergy for help. In story after story I was moved to tears of compassion."

Rabbi Zalman Schachter Shalomi, author of
The Geologist of the Soul

"Chaplains enter our lives at our most vulnerable moments. Their task isn't to cure but to heal: to create sacred space where we can find wholeness in the midst of our shattering. No one does this better then Reb Leon. The stories in Anatomy of a Tear carry on this work --- his work --- through the printed page. There is healing in this book if you dare to receive it."

Rabbi Rami Shapiro, author of
Perennial Wisdom for the Spiritually Independent

To Jackie:
My wife, my soul mate and my teacher,
who always grounds me, encourages my Chaplaincy work
and shares my joys and tears.

Contents

Section IV. Doing The Right Thing By Breaking Rules

Acknowledgements

I wish to acknowledge the many teachers who have enabled and given me permission to help others. From them I've learned the lessons that have enabled me to do my holy work embracing the language of the heart. I cannot possibly acknowledge everyone, so if your name is left out, please know that I hold you in my heart with the deepest gratitude.

To my wife Jackie, who continues to be my main inspiration. She believes in me, even when I do not believe in myself, and encourages me daily. She shares with me both my tears of sorrow, tears of joy and tears of unbound laughter.

To the thousands of people who invited me into their lives at their most vulnerable, critical and trying moments, trusting me with their innermost thoughts and fears.

To my teachers:

To Reb Zalman Schachter-Shalomi, who always encouraged me and taught me how to embrace the teachings of Torah through my heart.

To Reb Shlomo Carlebach, *z'l*, who taught me that the way to see what is in a person's heart is to look deep into their eyes, as well as the art of storytelling…and that laughter is so holy.

To Reb David Wolfe Blank, *z'l*, who believed in me and was my confidant and teacher. He made himself available to me on a weekly basis to study Torah, teaching me to how read between the lines.

To Rabbi Rami Shapiro, who by observance taught me the gift of presentation that enables me to share my point-of-view in a meaningful manner.

To Christine Macagli, my friend who checks in with me every day, and together we process our thoughts, techniques, and emotions as we head on out to work as hospice caregivers.

To Reverends Bob Jacoby, Jim Moon and Dan McRight whose examples as chaplains enhanced the way to perform my chaplaincy on a daily basis.

To Rabbi Goldie Milgram who encouraged me to share my stories through this book.

To Rabbi Miles Krassen, my soul brother, who was by my side as I began my journey, and continues to be present in my life.

To all the holy *schmoozers* I have met along the way.

To my holy children, Michael Olenick, Aliza Olenick, and Jenni Olenick and to my eleven grandchildren who continue to be my teachers on a daily basis, and always provide for me deep-belly laughs and even bigger smiles of the heart.

To Cheech, my dog, who sits at my side when returning from work and allows me to cuddle him as I meditate, reflect and process my day.

To the many "spell checkers" I blew up while writing my book.

To my editor, Amitai Zachary Malone, who made poetry of my words.

To editorial proof readers Judith Izen, Steven Crist, Jackie Olenick, and Michael Olenick.

…thank you all and may you all be blessed with the light of *Shechinah*!

THE HOLY BA'AL SHEM TOV once came upon one of his colleagues teaching the secret wisdom of Kabbalah (Jewish mysticism) in public. Later, in private, he chided his colleague for his way of teaching, saying, "You are teaching the literal words of the holy secrets to the people."

His colleague responded, "And you, Rebbe, don't you also teach the secret wisdom of Kabbalah to the masses?"

The Baal Shem Tov replied, "Yes, we both draw from the same source. But you teach it as it is written on the page of the book and I teach it as it applies to people in real life."

- Traditional, attributed to the Ba'al Shem Tov

Introduction

WE ARE FRAGILE. We vacillate between connection and disconnection to a higher power, to each other, and to ourselves. We walk the tightrope of life attempting to maintain our balance, hoping not to fall into the abyss of despair, depression, and habituation.

We are human and have been granted the gift of free choice. This gift is our ally if we embrace it. We can choose to live "the good life," fulfilling our hopes and dreams, through our thoughts and actions. But there are also times we feel we have lost our way and have been tossed aside by God and society. Sometimes we feel stuck in a black hole and, during such periods in our lives, however temporary, it is difficult to evolve. These feelings are not uncommon to any of us. However, we can break free from the chains of lethargy and despair with understanding, acceptance, and love.

It is my wish that the stories in this book will be a mirror to your innermost feelings. I invite you to connect with them in the tender spot in your heart and soul. Allow the stories that follow to penetrate through whatever layers in your heart that may subject your soul with undue grief, anger and even dismay so the healing process can begin.

From one perspective, a tear appears simple. Yet what flows from our eyes is, in actuality, the release of our emotions and feelings. In my years spent as a Chaplain I have realized that tears are not only a release, but also a complex manifestation. Each tear is as unique as a wave travelling across the ocean; like your fingerprint unlike any other.

A tear is a living vessel with its own anatomy. When we look at a diagram of the human body we see blood vessels, veins, arteries and muscle; Looking at its contents is like looking at a road map of how we exist. Our tears also contain an emotional road map of their own and the points of *this* map contain a story at each juncture. They are filled with a complex combination of grief, fear, laughter, anger and joy. These intersections made of tears encompass every emotion in our body, mind and spirit. Truly, these tears contain whole universes. My inspiration and my wish for *you* is that my stories lead you to the places that will inspire and enable you to fully embrace your emotions.

A bit about me...

I am a board certified chaplain. My job is to *be* with people when they are in crisis, whether physical, emotional, or spiritual. In such times I humbly and lovingly serve as a guide who listens, cares, and remains present. I aid in uncovering the apparent and hidden layers of grief, heartache, and fear that can be transformed and liberated while embodied and on your spiritual journey.

Together, through the stories present in this book, we can begin the process of peeling back the layers of fear and uncertainty so these feelings do not hold you back from most fully and joyfully living. Throughout I invite you to use the same methods I trained in, namely those of listening with compassion, seeking understanding, no matter the subject matter, remaining open to wisdom, and consistently returning to your ever-present ability to open your heart and listen to yourself and others as each new moment and experience arises. We were born with the natural gift to powerfully utilize these processes. Indeed, it is such loving and transformative methods that remain inherent and fundamental basics for our continued evolution.

I am dyslexic. Due to this, I read very slowly and I live with an impaired ability to retain certain types of specific information, as if magically, my brain transforms and morphs letters and numbers. As an adolescent I shed many tears of anger and frustration with my condition. However, I now view dyslexia as my gift. Throughout my life I have compensated with an enhanced ability to listen and observe. My listening has enabled me to connect to people and their situations with increased intuitive and observational skills, often times with an accuracy that has surprised myself as well as others.

At first this intuitive ability scared me and I did not claim this gift for myself for many years. As the years passed, however, I slowly embraced my intuitive ability, further trusting the unfolding process to accurately share these insights and feelings coming *through* me. I have learned that a *dis*-ability is not an *in*-ability and can either be a blessing or a curse. I chose the way of blessing and though there has been struggle, my life has been enriched because of it. My hope is to assist you in the realization that you can also benefit from your unique challenges, whatever they may be.

In my younger years I spent time on Columbia Avenue in North Philadelphia, near the campus of Temple University where I should have been attending classes. Instead, I chose to visit a pool hall located on the third floor over a luncheonette where I would purchase a lettuce sandwich on Wonder bread for five cents. I would sit down with my lettuce sandwich, quietly watching on as the men played pool, joked around and those playing began telling their street-wise stories. Here, I was the only white guy and easily the youngest in the room of mostly seventy-something year old men.

Most of my new friends wore slightly soiled double-breasted suits with wide neckties and though some were threadbare, each was elegant and regal in their own way. The room was hot and stuffy with fans overhead blowing years of dust around my feet and on to my sandwich. I would visit this poolroom daily.

Before long, I was accepted into their group and these men fast became my "comrades of the pool-hall." They began sharing their life stories and experiences directly with me. Perhaps it helped take them off guard I never held a pool stick in my hand? Nevertheless, I quietly marveled as I listened to their life adventures unfold, as if I had stepped into a secret myth-making society --- though these stories were real! The experiences related with this pool-hall grew into a knowledge that was a brilliant and unexpected educational experience. The characters I met and stories I heard were all about life, its challenges and battles, its defeats and glorious moments. It was about survival, and the endurance to create a quality life in what can sometimes be a cruel world. I cherished every moment and absorbed the stories like a sponge.

This was the first time I realized the gift of listening, and its blessing. I did not realize it at the time, but I was filling my "spiritual toolbox" with the tools of acceptance, listening and compassion --- all tools I would need decades later as I answered my vocational and spiritual call.

My wife calls me "a professional schmoozer," that is, I'm one who likes to talk with people. I love to discover folks I have never seen before and strike up a conversation, as we're all potential friends. I listen, I learn and I respond in kind. I do not have any prejudice about religion, skin color, ethnic background or beliefs in general. I truly believe we all emanate from the same Source and our diversity is our shared beauty.

My spiritual home is within Judaism and my spirituality is based on the Torah and its related teachings. I have studied many religions and have come to realize that religion is only a pathway to further open us up, the place in the heart where you can transcend all the forces that keep us paralyzed in fear, anger and impotence. This openness and acceptance is the universal key that unlocks the space, which is love. The stories you will read will reveal the importance of opening to such places in the heart without judgment.

My path to Chaplaincy was fated, and it is, in a sense, my *besheret*, or "soul-mate." When I tell people that I am both a rabbi and a chaplain and this is a second career, they often ask, "What did you do prior?" When I tell them I had built successful business trading pork in Bloomington, Indiana and Minnesota, their eyes open wide and their reaction is one typically mixed with equal parts amazement and incredulity, inspiring exclamations such as, "…*what?*"

The detours along the road to my ordination were blessings. I had to live in the "real world" and make a living; both further contributing to my "training," yet at the time, unbeknownst to me, the trajectory of my path was radically changing. In those early years when my children were growing, my responsibility of sustaining my family came first. My business took me to slaughterhouses, processing plants and truck stops. Even in such locales I was able to interact with the employees and listen to their stories. Having served in such ways, I understand the everyday stresses and concerns of people striving hard to make a living. I was also fortunate to meet with CEO's of major companies and sit in their boardrooms while making proposals for contracts. My interaction with all enabled me to see the great diversity of work-life and realize we all have a story, and each of our precious life stories contain lessons for our evolution, if we take the time to just *listen*. All that I was privileged to encounter over the years, the plethora and diversity of experiences, now stand out as examples of compassionate lessons and behavioral models.

During these years, I had my own company and I would arrive to my office by 5 a.m. By noon the pork trading business day was finished. I would return to my private office requesting my secretary to call me only if there was a problem. Then I would study with Rabbis and scholars around the country the rest of the day. So, it was thanks to the pork business I was able to earn my ordination! Sometimes a path to your goals takes you in a direction that may seem totally opposite of what you expect.

One of the stories that I share below is titled "Reincarnation." This event transpired when I was in the hospital sitting with one of my children who had a mysterious, undiagnosed condition. It was this specific event detailed in this story, and my ability to aid someone in desperate need, that put me on the path, unknown to me at the time, to answer the call of becoming a chaplain.

There are numerous books detailing the many techniques on healing, grief and how to embrace one's feelings. I believe the path to healing and acceptance is an individual trait and the formula for "going on with life" after a trauma needs to be addressed on a case-by-case basis. We are all different and we all grieve and heal in our own way. My role as a chaplain is to help you recognize your specific needs and send you on a path of healing, moving forward after suffering whatever trauma disturbed your life.

My wish is these stories from my life experiences help free you to process and eventually embrace your emotions, delineating emotion in general from fear, specifically. If we can free ourselves from the fundamental fears of loneliness, anger, and neglect, preventing fear itself, we can then proceed with life its pleasures and joy, further evolving and increasing the quality of life for both ourselves as well as for others.

Life can be like walking on a tightrope and we are able to learn the balance necessary to not fall into the abyss. We are on this tightrope, so to speak, like a bird on a wire: we can fall off or fly away to safety. The safety I'm speaking of is the understanding that we need not suffocate ourselves with grief, fear, and pity. We can free ourselves enough to go to a safe place of realizing that life, although sometimes cruel, affords us the opportunities to become stronger. As you read my stories, I invite you to recall your own stories. The lessons for each of us, coming from our very lives, are hidden beneath the layers that make up our experience.

I have realized through my dyslexia that we must listen not only to the people and situations that surround us, but also to our self. Life's detours that we feel *dis*-able us can actually *en*-able us and become a blessing. It is stated in the Torah, "You can be a blessing or a curse, be a blessing, choose life." I often think about this teaching and the related, potential blessings that may at first appear to us in the form of "a curse." Ultimately, I believe many of our blessings come from our empowered choice to engage life-changing situations and by attaining wisdom from them. I am optimistic each story you read will ignite a flame in your heart, a touchstone, inquiring how it may relate to your own life and how you may best learn from it. In this way, our sharing of stories increases our emotional and life experience evolution, together.

I've achieved several ordinations in my life, including board certification as a chaplain. However, the ordination I cherish the most is *Ba'al HaBracha* (lit., "Master of the Holy Blessing"). I know that through actively giving blessings the paths for healing are open, and we can choose to travel these paths. As part of chaplaincy training, we are taught to pray with families or individuals in need. I do this only when specifically requested. I feel that channeling a blessing ascends to a high spiritual sphere and creates a direct pathway to the Holy One. That is, a specific blessing with proper intention touches the heart of the receiver, uplifting them out of a space of fear or chaos --- a space where they are confined.

I have been asked many times, "How does one bless?" The answer has to come from inside the deepest, most authentic and, thus, vulnerable space in your heart. We can also begin to learn this blessing activity from the masters and mediums of this beautiful method. For example, I remember a time when Rabbi Shlomo Carlebach, *z'l* was giving a blessing to my wife, Jackie.

Reb Shlomo began his blessing by saying to her, "You are the holiest person in the universe." Jackie responded, "Reb Shlomo, you say that to everyone." Reb Shlomo replied, "Yes, Jackie, but I am looking into *your* eyes now." It's this realization, namely that *you* are a unique blessing in the universe, that, once realized, may be the greatest gift you can give yourself and then, that you give to others.

Recently, driving, I saw what appeared to be a homeless man holding a sign that read, "Hungry, please help." I gave him some money for a meal. He leaned in the window with his unshaven, dirty face, disheveled hair and offered me a strong blessing. He said, "I bless you and your family never to have to stand on a street corner begging, like I, and I bless you with the abundance of life." This blessing was so beautiful and moved me so deeply I cried. So, as you read the stories I encourage you to look into the window of your soul and bless yourself. As I wept upon hearing the holy beggar's blessing, so shall you, when the blessing received or given is authentic. Sometimes, however, the blessing is not verbal.

One such silent blessing I received was while I was visiting a patient in a hospice unit. I saw a tiny, 95 year old woman with sagging, wrinkled skin, her face shriveled and drawn. Her forearm was conspicuous with the blue tattooed numbers that forever mark a concentration camp survivor. As I leaned over her bed and our eyes met, she lifted her bony, tiny hands and stroked my face and beard with a gentleness that a mother would use to caress her infant child. I knew that she was blessing me through her eyes and with her tender touch. Although she could not speak, she knew that I was also blessing her. She was receiving the blessing via the language of our hearts. When I got up to leave, she clutched my hand, a non-verbal signal telling me, "please don't leave me alone." I remained with her until she fell asleep.

Life is a great journey, and each day a new beginning. I offer you a blessing to read the stories with an open heart and to allow the stories to open your path to healing and new beginnings of your own!

May all who read this book gain insight from the holy One of Blessing to open their hearts and souls to God, the Universe, themselves, and each other. Amen!

- Leon Olenick

Section I.

Witnessing Miracles

WE ALL HAVE MIRACLES in our lives happening on a daily basis however sometimes we do not recognize they are miracles. It is my hope the stories in this section may serve as a template, supporting you to learn how to listen to your inner thoughts and recognize the miracles in your daily lives, inviting them out of the depths of the unconscious and into the light of your awareness.

Reincarnation

MANY OF US who are having serious physical problems or are facing death wonder and then ask me where their soul will go. They are at least curious and frightened. They want to know what happens next. Though I cannot answer this question, occasionally we catch glimpses of the beyond. For example, we hear stories and wonder how the tale might affect us in our daily lives. Then, often times when we least expect it, the answer comes to us like a bolt of lightning on a clear day. I invite you to read the following story with a gentle awareness that over time, the clarity may come into an even greater focus.

Even those who are not facing terminal illness, the question of reincarnation enters our psyche. We want to know if there is life beyond death. There is no clear answer to this question. Some people feel the experiencing of *déjà vu* is from a past lifetime. Some psychologists or spiritual practitioners attempt to take us back to a past life as a tool for healing. However, any concrete proof about reincarnation evades us and confounds scientists and psychics alike. We are curious about life after death, however focusing all our attention and energy on this issue, detracts us from living our lives as fully as we can, moment to moment, in the present.

AS A CHAPLAIN, I am consistently asked if there is life after death. We all want to know what happens to our soul after death. Additionally, patients and families generally want to know if I believe reincarnation exists as a possibility. I tell them I am not sure, and that no one can totally and completely know. I believe in the word *beshert*, which, translated, means "meant to be."

One of my children was very ill. She was bleeding internally. The doctor placed her in the hospital for tests in order to determine the cause of the bleeding. She was a toddler. After many tests and several days, the doctor told my wife and I that he had not yet determined the cause, and he had to perform more tests. He said if the test came back positive, he would have to perform a serious surgery that would endanger her life. My wife and I were worried and nervous - we stayed at the hospital for the night.

The evening prior to the test, my wife went home to shower and have some rest. I spent the night at the hospital alone. Hospitals can be very dreary at night. The fluorescent lights are turned down, giving off an alien glow and the bustling activity of the daytime staff shifts with the relative tranquility of the night staff. As our senses are elevated, the odor of a hospital intensifies. It is a very quiet atmosphere. The echoes of the hallway outweighed any other sound. The feeling of pain, agony and restlessness permeates the physical space.

I sat with my daughter until she fell asleep and summoned the four archangels --- Michael, Gabriel, Uriel and Rafael --- to protect her as I chanted what is called "The Bedtime Shema." After she was in a deep sleep, I decided to leave the room and sit in the lounge for a while.

It was midnight when I entered the lounge. It was very sterile. The furniture was stained and showed signs of significant wear. You could feel the mix of love, fear, joy, and delight in the very furniture, as if these very chairs told the story of the people who sat here before me. The magazines were old and disheveled and the walls were painted the same uninspiring color as the hospital rooms. The lights were dimmed here, as well, and it was, actually, relatively peaceful as I was the only person present.

I had just begun to doze when a woman walked into the room. I nodded in her direction but even I, the "schmoozer," was not up for conversation at the moment. We sat together in the room, silent, for about an hour. She appeared almost thirty years old, dressed in jeans and a faded T-shirt, unassuming throughout. However, her face was overcome with fear.

Eventually she looked directly at me and said, "My son is dying for my sins". I did not respond. She repeated, "My son is dying for my sins." Her tone amplified until it became a piercing shrill as she wailed. She rose out of her chair and then immediately fell to the floor, weighed down by an invisible yet profound *gravitas*, continuing to scream the same words. She became wild and out of control, rolling and writhing all over the floor of the room.

I fell to my knees and attempted to calm her. She was strong and I was forced to wrestle her into a place of relative calm. As she responded to my attempts to comfort and console her, she regaining her composure, we moved to the sofa. I introduced myself and inquired how I could be of further help. Her name was Judy and she repeated, "My son is dying for my sins." Through acknowledging and encouraging her to share, I gave her the much needed space to tell her story, heart-wrenching as it was.

"My son, Joshua, has terminal cancer. He is seven years old. The doctor said there is no hope for him and he will die within a month." She continued as tears flowed from her eyes. "I was divorced about a year ago. My former husband was abusive and I was happy to be rid of him. I felt caged for our entire marriage and when I was free I acted out. I used drugs and slipped into a habit of heavy drinking."

"I loved to party," she admitted. "I went out until wee hours of the morning, slept with many men…I can't even count them. I was a party girl and I loved every minute of it. However, I have now since stopped that life. I have a job and I am off both drugs and alcohol."

"In the meantime, my son Joshua became ill. He was diagnosed with a stage four cancer. The doctor said there is no hope --- and he is going to die. I know it's because of the lifestyle I led. I was such a mess…"

I thought of the teaching that our children will suffer for our sins. I do not believe in this teaching and believe that we all live our own lives.

Although not yet trained in Chaplaincy work, I deduced this was her way of initiating the grieving process related to the loss she suffered after her divorce. Grief comes forth in various ways and attracts from all directions, sometimes quite powerfully and completely. This process can be cruel and overwhelming. I later realized that lifestyle changes can, of themselves, invite grief, and her particular way of grieving, even though she was in an abusive relationship, had emerged in this seemingly spontaneous manner.

I sat with my arm around her searching for the proper consoling and supportive words. My shirt was wet from her tears. At this point in my life I knew only one Hasidic story, as I was a novice in study and practice. I asked her if I might tell her this story. Now calm and us having established a bit of rapport, she agreed.

This story takes place in a small village in Europe, about two hundred years ago. There was a butcher and he was preparing to close his shop for Shabbat. He had one chicken left in his meat case. He believed it was kosher, however there was a bit of doubt. Selling this chicken would afford him a profit for the day rather than a loss, but the question remained, was this chicken fully kosher?

Just then, a woman walked into the shop, right before closing time. All she needed was a chicken and as she inspected the one chicken left, she asked, "Is this chicken kosher?"

He hesitated. "Uh…" eventually stammering out, "of course it is kosher!" Naturally, she purchased the chicken and left, heading home to celebrate Shabbat with her family.

About three years later the butcher died. Several more years after that, a boy was born in the village. He was born deaf and blind, and had no working limbs --- it was a miracle he even survived birth. Anyway, at this time the mother of the crippled boy was in a quandary and sought answers. In those times people would travel to the Rabbi for advice and guidance for difficult situations. She gained an audience with The Ba'al Shem Tov, a name that means, "Master of the Holy Name," and, as it should turn out, he is able to see into the past, the future and the secrets of the present.

His given name was Israel and he is unquestionably the historical father of Hasidic thought and practice. He was quite unlike the rabbis of today. He traveled from town to town and told stories to people. All of his stories had a specific lesson which also served as a remedy to a person's particular needs, whether the individual was aware of this need or not. He dressed in bright color clothes and was easily identified and remained quite approachable.

The woman told the Ba'al Shem Tov her story, describing the little boy who now lay lifeless in his crib at home. The Ba'al Shem Tov listened intently and, nodding, said, "Continue to care for him as you have been doing. I will visit your home on his third birthday."

The years went by and the woman continued to care for her son, as she had been, as prescribed by this holy man. She loved her son deeply, with all her heart.

On his third birthday the entire town was gathered in front of the home of the woman and boy anticipating the arrival of the Ba'al Shem Tov. As he exited his wagon you could feel the excitement building to a crescendo.

He passed the crowd carrying a paper bag and as he approached the crib of the boy, he opened the bag and pulled a chicken from it.

He asked the boy, "Is this chicken kosher?"

The blind, deaf boy looked up and replied, "I don't know!" Upon saying these words the boy closed his eyes and died.

The boy's mother screamed with terror and grief. The son she had grown to love so much was dead. Her son's end is what she remained hopeful for?

The Ba'al Shem Tov sat with her and explained. He told her of the butcher who had died many years ago. He explained that this butcher's soul went through many incarnations and had been, indeed, a very holy soul.

He explained that our souls, after death, choose a body that it needs to complete the *mitzvot* (good deeds) it has not completed in the previous body. He went on to say that very few souls ever complete all the *mitzvot*. He told her if a soul does, in fact, complete all the *mitzvot* it does not have to come back. "But," he stressed, "this is very rare and usually does not happen."

He went on to say when the soul does come back it tends to make more mistakes. This is God's way, the reason we have not had a new soul for thousands of years. This particular butcher's soul, however, was so holy that it had completed all the *mitzvot*, but by not telling the woman he was not sure if the chicken was fully kosher, he violated the last one *mitzvot* he could have completed and had to come back, taking another body.

The Ba'al Shem Tov clarified, "If the Holy One of Blessing sent him back in a healthy body, he would no doubt violate more. So, he was sent back in a form that he was unable to accomplish this. You were destined with the privilege of caring for and loving this soul until the proper time for it to be ultimately released. You are a very holy woman and this is why we may celebrate and not simply mourn."

Clutching Judy's hand tightly I explained, "We have no idea why Joshua is going to die. There can be many reasons. Maybe his mission on Earth was complete and you were chosen to nurture and love him."

I then asked, "Have you ever heard of the Ba'al Shem Tov?"

She looked deeply into my eyes, her hands shaking almost out of control, and said, "He was my great-great-great-grandfather. I have been told that Joshua is a direct descendent from the line of his daughter, Fayga."

I sat, stunned and utterly speechless.

In the early morning my wife arrived at the hospital. The doctor approached us and declared, "I do not have a medical explanation, however, all the bleeding has stopped. You may take your daughter home today."

The months passed, and Joshua died. Judy, with the help of my wife, contacted the Hasidic rabbi in our area. Joshua was indeed the tenth direct descendent of the Ba'al Shem Tov. She became active in the *schul* ("synagogue") and, last we heard, was observing Shabbat and living a happy, healthy life.

My wife and I believe our daughter was the designate, sent to the hospital in order for us to meet this particular woman and tell this particular story.

Is the story true? I do not know. I do know that at this time and place the words were placed in my *neshama* ("soul") to share with her. Is there reincarnation? Hopefully. But, may we all have a long wait to discover this for ourselves!

As I said in the beginning of the story, I believe in the word "*besheret*" (lit., "meant to be"). I believe I was placed in the room with Judy to tell her this story. I also believe my daughter was the innocent messenger to bring me there. We all find ourselves in situations that we do not understand or can make sense of. This creates fear, as we are creatures of habit, and want all in life to "be as planned." The question is how and when must we surrender and realize that our path to what we need or desire may not come as planned. My thought and blessing is to embrace our situations and know that a life experience will come in ways we do not expect, nor comprehend as we are going through it. I believe the Holy One of Blessing places us where we must be.

Darkness To Light

LIFE IS PRECIOUS. We attempt to maintain a healthy life and live long, contributing to our Universe. We have children, we raise them, protect them and pray daily for their well-being. There are times in my Chaplaincy that a mother or father, after losing a child will ask, "Why did they die?" A parent is not supposed to bury a child. The grief and disappointment in their eyes and deepest part of their soul tells of their unfathomable loss. What happens when one of the parents loves and wants to nourish the child and the other does not, or cannot? What happens when both parents love and cherish the child? This story will take you on a twisting path of love, expectations, tragedy and redemption that reveal our responsibility to our vulnerable and innocent children.

IT WAS SATURDAY NIGHT and three stars peeked through the clear California sky. It was time to bid farewell to Shabbat for another week. Jackie and I prepared for the departure of this Shabbat with the *Havdalah* ceremony.

We lit the braided candle, which reminds us how our lives are braided with our Universe and with one another. The flame accentuated the light in our eyes. We poured a cup of wine, serving to remind us of deep wisdom, and sniffed the fragrance of the spice that Jackie prepared to summon a sweet week, a week to balance both inner and outer *shalom*, or, "peace." We sang the traditional blessings, as well as adding our own blessings for those we love and even for those we sometimes experience as harder to love. We summoned Elijah, the prophet, and Miriam, the prophetess, to join with us in our attempt to heal those in need through these prayers. We hugged and stood silently after extinguishing the flame, soaking in an invisible light that remained with us.

We typically go to a movie on Saturday night, or visit with friends, however on this particular evening I was "on-call" at the hospital, so we remained home. I did not like serving my time on-call: The beeper I was required to monitor would routinely startle me with its alarm, as if crying out "someone is in trouble!"

We decided to have a simple dinner and listen to some music while talking with each other. Thus far, it was appearing to be an enjoyably calm night. We were listening to Nina Simone as she sang, "There's a new day coming…" and then it came: *Beep! Beep! Beep!* We looked at each other with a frown as I fumbled with the rude device. Our evening together was coming to an end. I called into the hospital and was told I was needed in the pediatric unit. I did not know the nature of the emergency, but I knew right away that a child was in danger.

It was about 10 p.m. when I arrived. The halls at a hospital in the evening after visiting hours are especially gloomy. Shadows are everywhere adding to the heart-wrenching echoes of little voices crying for help. I went to the charge nurse to inquire about the call I'd received. She was pale with fear and anger. She told me that a three-year old baby had been brutally shaken by his father because the child would not quiet down. She said the police had the father in custody, and the mother and grandmother were in the room with the baby. The physician was present and told me that the baby boy had no brain function and was on life support. He requested I report the test results to the mother, and he would be present to explain the medical terms.

It was as if this particular night, my world with it, was turned upside-down. I felt the light in my soul created by the serene *havdalah* candle being extinguished. The prayer I said only a short while ago, for people we love and people we do not love, felt wholly negated.

"How could I pray for a 'man,' such as this that would do this to his own innocent child?" I was triggered and I wanted to shake this man as he did to his own child. I had to excuse myself and found a corner to be alone for a moment. All I could do was pray.

"*Ribono Shel Olam*, 'Master of the Universe,' You showered me with the delight of Your Shabbat. You created in me calm, delight and unity in the deepest part of my soul, but look at me now! I am now full of anger and hatred! Please, grant me the wisdom I asked for as I sipped the blessed wine. I need Your help to remain compassionate and strong to be an aid for this little boy and his mother. Let the correct words --- Your words --- come to me from the depths of my heart. Remove this feeling of hostility I'm feeling now from this act against one of Your babies."

I entered the room, and saw the mother, Miriam, sitting on a rocking chair. She was dressed in the same nightgown that she had intended to sleep peacefully in that night. She was rocking back and forth, clearly in shock. Her rocking was like a mantra pleading for help from the Universe, not unlike the *shuckling*, or swaying movements of *hasidim* as they fervently pray.

The salt of dried tears covered each and every part of her puffy face creating a tender mask of horror. The strands of her long red hair were wild and hung without direction. Her face was bruised, and small cuts peeked through her tears. In the bed attached to a machine with tubes and wires protruding from his little arms lay Simon. He was motionless and I could feel the presence of the angel of death.

I did not bother to introduce myself as I approached Miriam. I simply took her in my arms and held her. It was clear her shock and grief were beyond the necessities of language at this time. Her heart pressed upon my heart as our tears created a stream of togetherness in this profoundly sad moment. As we embraced I felt as if we were being enveloped in the loving embrace of the *Shechinah* (the Feminine aspect of The Divine), also escorting Simon to the waiting angels.

We sat together, silent, for a long time. Eventually I asked the kind doctor to leave. It felt as if he was serving in a clinical capacity, one which felt immeasurably cold at the time, as if he only wanted to make his report, getting this over with and go home. However, it was not the time for clock-watching, so to speak, as time had functionally stopped. When the energy felt right and it appeared there was an appropriate opening, I shared with Miriam the report: Simon had passed. She already knew the devastating truth in her heart and was not shocked, but further numbed to hear it said aloud. We cried some more.

Tears, they are as if our inner *mikveh* ("ritual bath"), baths us from the inside-out. Our tears are so precious as they cleanse our sorrow, relieve our pain and even mark our joy. We draw water from the well of our soul through liberating our tears.

I chose not to address the violence of her husband, making what would have only amounted to a futile attempt to explain why he did what he did. This was not the time for such conversations. My focus was solely on being present with Miriam and the lifeless body of Simon.

I requested the doctor return so he could convey the medical terms to this grieving mother, which he did. By this time, my shirt was soaked with Miriam's tears of despair and heartache.

In my Chaplaincy training, I was taught the compassionate way of approaching the subject of organ donation when a death was imminent and I knew the time had come to address this issue with Miriam. I asked Miriam if she considered donating the healthy organs of Simon. I explained that maybe another child could live and be partners with Simon in our Universe.

Her eyes partially lit up, as if she liked this thought and was agreeing with the possibility. In fact, I believe this option of Simon contributing to another child's chance at life restored some glint of hope in her soul. I immediately called the transplant team in, as this is a matter that must transpire in a timely fashion. This team at the hospital was comprised of wonderful, loving individuals, filled with empathy and understanding. They explained the procedure to Miriam, providing details about how Simon's body would be handled with the utmost sensitivity, loving kindness, respect and dignity. She was content with this option and they began their preparation. Around this time Miriam's sister arrived and I took the opportunity to take a short walk outside to breathe some fresh air and reinvigorate my inner resourcefulness. The moon was disappearing over the western horizon as the sun was begging to break through the night's darkness to the east. A new day was dawning and, I thanked God for the renewal of the light each day!

As I regained my breath and began to say my morning prayers, *it* came again: *Beep! Beep! Beep!* I was rattled and reminded I was still on-call, just as I was regaining my sense of orientation. I returned to the hospital, answering the page. I was told there was an emergency in the Pediatric Unit and they needed me immediately. A bit frayed from the previous crisis that had me up all night, my first reaction was, "What? How can that be? I was already there…" In fact, the nurse informing me of my next duty confirmed room 103 in the Pediatric Unit urgently needed me.

Upon entering the room I found a little girl of only five years facing imminent death due to liver failure. Her blond curls were pulled back to make room for the oxygen to flow into her mouth. The poles supporting the intravenous tubes were filled to capacity dangling with life saving medications. Her mother and father appeared exhausted. Their faces were filled with hope and worry.

The family had just been informed prior to my arrival that a liver had been located and a transplant would be performed in but moments. They wanted me to pray for success and to offer hope and thanks, which, of course, I did, though thoroughly exhausted and then they shared with me their story.

Sara was their only child. Due to complicated birth issues they could not have any more children through natural means. They spoke about how much they loved Sara, and about the light she brought to their lives. They told me about how she was a prankster who would make them laugh all the time, and how they knew deep in their hearts if she could live she would contribute to our world in uniquely beautiful ways.

As the surgical team entered the room to prepare Sara, I let the parents know I would return very shortly. I went around the corner to check on Miriam.

I knew the liver for Sara was coming from Simon, however confidentiality laws (the protocols of HIPAA) forbade me from sharing this information.

I entered Simon's room. The shades were drawn and darkness enveloped all space. I was informed it would be about an hour before the team was ready. The family was reminiscing about some of Simon's little tricks and quirks as I left again, respecting their private space.

I turned the corner into Sara's room. Contrasted with the room Miriam and the body of Simon occupied, here the room was filled with a sense of hope and delight. The early morning light was shining on Sara's small face through the nearby window. I stayed for a while as the family shared more stories about Sara. Soon after the pager rang and I was informed the transplant team was ready and I was summoned back into Simon's room. I asked his mother and relatives now present to surround the bed and hold hands as we prayed. The transplant team and floor nurse joined us:

"Holy One of Blessing, we stand before you with Simon, your little warrior. His mission in this Universe is about to come to an end and we place his soul with You. As he goes back to Your Cosmic Embrace, let him be met by the same familiar angel that accompanied him when he came from Your Womb so he is not afraid. Let his mother rest knowing that his life, although so short, has had deep meaning and made a profound and unique difference in Your Universe. Send your angel of healing to his mama's heart, that she may be able to embrace the bitterness it now holds. Let the other children who are to receive his organs live long lives and create peace in the World. God, we release Your angel. Amen."

As they took Simon from the room, I embraced Miriam, her mother and sister as we all sobbed, saying goodbye. I knew, as I walked them to the door, I would probably never see Miriam or her family again, however they have made a deep, everlasting impression upon my soul. I turned the corner and proceeded to return to Sara's room just as she was being placed on the gurney to be taken to surgery. I joined hands with her parents, as I just had with Miriam and her family only moments ago.

"God, we place the *neshama* (lit., "soul") of Sara with You. She is one of Your precious little ones who brings joy to her parents and the Your world. Guide the surgeon's hands as she replaces the liver of this precious child. Allow her body to accept this liver and perform its function of filtering out all of the poison from her system. Let her soul know that she has been doubly blessed. Let her *neshama* filter out any and all negative energy from the Universe. Let her live a long life in peace and harmony with You. Let her partner with the soul of her donor. Amen."

I waited with Sara's parents until the surgery was complete. During this time I spoke of the importance of prayer for the soul of the person that donated the liver, a teaching I learned from my teacher and *Rebbe*, Rabbi Zalman Schachter-Shalomi. I suggested that each time they pray or meditate, they should remember the soul of the donor, and that these prayers send sparks of energy to that particular soul so that it can be free to complete its particular journey. They agreed and acknowledged the inherent beauty in this process and shared they would pray daily for this unknown person and would encourage Sara do the same when she was old enough to understand.

The doctor eventually returned and announced the transplant was a success and that Sara was doing well. I hugged her parents in both joy and deep relief as they celebrated.

I again walked outside the hospital and sat on a bench under a beautiful California oak tree that protected me from the sun. I reached for my cell phone and called Jackie. I asked her to pick me up. She reminded me that I had my own car. I said "I know, however I cannot drive home." She fetched me. When she pulled up, I was still sitting on the bench. Tears were streaming from my eyes. I could not shut them off. She did not ask me what happened. There would be time for this later. She held me, and cried with me. She placed me in the car, took me home, and guided me to our bed.

As I lay in bed, my heart was pounding. I thought of how God had created the souls of these babies, and now their bodies would be inextricably linked. Was it a divine plan to create this togetherness, or only a coincidence? I do not know. I do know that we are all in one way or another dependent on each other, and we do not stand alone.

We live in the age where organ donation saves lives. Not long ago this was a mere theory and many religions were against it. Unfortunately, some continue to condemn this life saving procedure. I have been taught, through my study of Torah, "if you save one life, you save the entire world." This practice is now widely accepted and encouraged. If you wish to donate your organs, you must make your wishes known by arrangements in your Advanced Directive, or checking the box on your Driver's License. This tells your loved ones, unambiguously, of your desire to perform your final *mitzvah*. We now have a new challenge in our society. This challenge is the issue of "stem cell research." We are facing the same roadblocks we faced prior to the acceptance of organ donation. We see our brothers and sisters debilitated with conditions that can possibly be cured or contained if our society and more importantly, the legislature, accepts this research. My hope is that our constricted archaic views will be set aside and we embrace the gift of this healing technology.

I drifted off to sleep visualizing these two holy children skipping together holding hands.

From Slumber To Life

THE SOUNDS OF DIFFERENT FORMS of music move through us with the capacity to open our hearts.

During the Hebrew month of *Elul*, we sound the *shofar* daily. In ancient times the piercing blast of the *shofar* was sounded to inform the Israelites that it was time to pack their belongings and move on. It was also used to announce a significant event. My teacher, Rabbi David Wolfe-Blank, *z'l*, taught me that the sound of the *shofar* penetrates our being and enables us to receive a direct spark of life from the Holy One. It is as if a holy internal lightning bolt wakes us up. The following is a story of a young man awakening in such a way.

MOISHE, THE TEENAGE SON OF A FRIEND, was living near our home while attending school, which happened to be quite far from where his parents lived. Rosh Hashanah (the Jewish holiday celebrating New Year) was approaching. We called and invited him to spend the holiday with us, as he was living with a family that was not Jewish. Moishe told us he was going to skip services this year, that he had a football game, explaining how much more important it was that he be at the game instead of services. My wife promptly got on the phone and said, in her direct yet loving way, "You are *not* going to skip Rosh Hashanah! Get your *tuchas* on a bus and be here in time for dinner...*followed by services!*"

After attempting every rationalization and presenting all the arguments he could think up, he agreed to come. Entering our home we were able to see the disappointment in his face at missing the game. He was a large young man. He had huge arms and hands, gigantic feet, hair that was long and wild, and a smile that could melt the coldest of hearts. We were very close to him, as he had lived with us for about a year. He was sensitive, intelligent and funny --- a gentle giant from an observant Jewish home. He was in the midst of his teenage rebellion against the established Jewish community and his parents' values.

We lit candles and recited the traditional prayers. He spoke to his family and wished them a good year, and received a blessing from his father. We enjoyed our holiday dinner, sang, and spoke about the meaning of the New Year. We discussed the word *teshuva* --- returning --- that is usually translated as repentance. We spoke about what we were returning to: our universe, ourselves, and the roots of our being were the general consensus that night. We also spoke about being able to hear the blasts of the *shofar* the next day. The one hundred blasts would break down all the barriers between us and God, between each other, and even within ourselves. The blasts would prompt us to action and awaken us from the slumber of our daily habitual routines.

Moishe was attentive and respectful, but not overjoyed. We went to sleep and then traveled to the synagogue in the morning. The Temple was filled with a joyful spirit, music, singing, and dancing. People were hugging and wishing each other a good year, offering the blessing that they be inscribed in the book of life for the coming year. When the Torah was taken from the ark, it was passed around the congregation. The joy and melody that accompanied it released our souls and opened our hearts. Moishe was not moved. He sat quietly. I believe his mind may have been on the football field. While the Torah was out of the ark the *Ba'al T'kiyah*, the person who sounds the *shofar*, was called up. He held the most beautiful ram's horn under his arm. It was about three feet long, and had waves of curls. We all stood as the *shofar* began to sound:

The blasts were crisp, clear and penetrated the through to the souls of all present. I felt my heart opening up, inspired for a year of renewal. I felt whole; I felt at peace.

The final blast lasted what seemed like a couple of minutes. The sound filled the room for what could have been hours. We were joined as one with our ancestors. The service was high and, as it concluded, those gathered hugged and kissed and blessed one another for a good year as they left the Temple.

Moishe asked if we were going to go home now. We shared with him our custom was to visit a hospital after Rosh Hashanah services to sound the *shofar* for patients too ill --- often times, terminally --- to leave for the holiday. Usually, patients who were able, left the hospital for such services. Upon entering the hospital, I asked Moishe if he would be my *Ba'al T'kiya,* my *shofar* blower. He agreed. I handed the *shofar* to him, and he tucked it under his arm.

The first room we entered was home to an elderly woman lying motionless in bed. Her aid told us that she was comatose. We asked if we may sound the *shofar.* She agreed. I recited the blessing and Moishe sounded three blasts. I then called for a final blast of power and sustained length. Moishe blew and the woman, previously comatose, opened her eyes and sat up. All in the room were astounded.

I have been taught that when a person is comatose they are able to hear everything around them. Hearing, in fact, is the last sense to leave the body as a person comes close to death. For this reason, I often ask families of a comatose patient to sit at their bedside and recite a *"heshbon hanefesh,"* an accounting of the soul, to clear up any obstacles that have come between them in order for the person to leave the world peacefully, and the family member to have peace and closure after their death. I believe that when the *shofar* sounded the woman was taken back to all the years she heard the *shofar* in her lifetime and she knew the Holy One was calling her home.

After visiting several rooms, Moishe's demeanor was visibly shifting. Moishe's eyes were starting to light up and I noticed a marked sense of satisfaction on his face. He was no longer agitated, angry, fidgety and moment by moment, he was maturing before my eyes.

Upon entering the last room of the day we found a man of about eighty years. He was sitting in bed with his *tallit* (prayer shawl) draped over him. His *siddur* (prayer book) was on the table next to him, within reach.

"Hello Mr. Bloom, my name is Leon. Would you permit me to sound the *shofar* blasts for you?" His eyes looked from the book. "I am not Mr. Bloom. I am *Chazzan* Bloom, a cantor. Please come in." I asked permission to also invite Moishe and Jackie in, and he agreed. Upon our entering, he began to share with us.

"I have been a cantor all my life. This is the first Rosh Hashanah that I have not been on the pulpit. I have throat cancer and I am stuck here. Just now I was praying, "*Ribono Shel Olam*, Master of the Universe, please allow me to hear the *shofar* blast this year. I do not know if I will be here next year and my *neshama* longs for the sweet sounds." Then, the three of you appear here, in my room! You are not here by chance, young man," Chazzan Bloom said to Moishe. "God has brought you to me."

I asked Moishe if he was ready. He nodded, and I called for the first blast.

"*Wait!*" shouted Chazzan Bloom. "You did not yet offer the blessing!" I apologized and explained that we had done the blessing many times this day and I was sorry that I was remiss. He said that he would chant the blessing. He took a deep breath and in his finest cantorial voice began to chant the traditional prayer. He was singing to God. It was as if his soul was being visited by the thousands of congregants for whom he sang over the many years he served in services at the temple. When his recitation of the blessing was almost complete, his voice broke off. His face showed anguish and his eyes filled with tears as he started to panic. Fear seemed to settle over him as he realized the severity of his throat cancer --- it was literally stealing his words, his voice, his life.

Moishe rushed to his side, took the book and said, "Please allow me to finish the prayer." Moishe finished the prayer and sounded the shofar blasts with the energy of a heavenly angel. Chazzan Bloom thanked us for coming and asked Moishe to come close. He placed his hands on Moishe's head and, with tearful eyes and an open heart, recited the priestly blessing in Hebrew and English.

"May God bless you and keep you. May God's Presence shine upon you and be gracious to you. May God's Presence be with you and grant you peace." He then kissed him on the cheek.

We bid Chazzan Bloom a Happy New Year, I offered a prayer for healing) and, with that, we left the hospital.

Once we were outside, Moishe paused. With tears streaming down his face, he looked at Jackie and me and said, "I now know the meaning of *teshuva*."

We are sent to the places we are most needed. Sometimes we resist the call, let alone the lessons we must get to know in order to evolve in our Universe. Moishe's soul and Chazzan Bloom's soul joined together on this particular occasion, an unexpected blessing for them both. I have a sense that the Holy One of Blessing, and angels, witnessed this meeting and blessed them both. They were both blessed with "returning", each on their own path --- one of a path of getting ready to leave the world and one getting ready to enter the world as a fully developed young man.

The Shock

THE DISEASE THAT IS MOST MISUNDERSTOOD because its symptoms are not physically visible is mental illness. As a boy growing up, in my world, mental illness was not mentioned in my family, as it was a *shandah* ("a shameful thing"). Thankfully, in our age, we recognize mental illness and place it in the same category as any other debilitating and deteriorating illness. We now know there are designer meds that can be tweaked for a patient's needs and enable them to live a "normal" life. We also know that sometimes, it is not meds that are needed, but an insightful counselor who can see to the root of the patient's symptoms and help alleviate pain and suffering.

I WAS ASSIGNED TO SERVE IN THE PSYCHIATRIC WARD at a hospital as part of my residency training as a chaplain. I was excited about this three-month rotation as most chaplains are not permitted in such units. We have all seen various movies about the Psych wards depicting horror stories. Kesey's "One Flew Over the Cuckoo's Nest," with Jack Nicholson is a poignant example. I was surprised to find out that in real life these units are indeed scary and sometimes torturous places.

On the first day in the unit my task was to simply get acquainted with where I was to be spending my time. I was introduced to staff and warned not to listen to the majority of patients as they were manipulative and did not know what they really wanted. "Just shake your head, agree, and ignore them," I was told repetitively. "That way," I was advised, "you will not have to converse with them." The nurses in the unit seemed hardened, no doubt by their experiences in the very place I was now a resident-in-training at, and I could tell that some had lost their compassion and patience. I sat in on some groups and observed the goings-on as best I could. It was an eye-opening and ultimately uninspiring first day.

The following day I was invited to visit certain patients to attempt to satisfy their spiritual needs. I listened and observed. My intention was to internalize the various situations before drawing any conclusions and determining my road to proceed with spiritual care. I saw individuals who acted out and were, at times, visibly over-medicated so they would quiet down. I saw others who were attempting to speak their mind, craving to simply be heard, all the while being ignored, day in and day out. Again I was told, "don't listen to them, Leon. They only speak gibberish." Their eyes, the windows unto their soul, were informing me of a wholly different story.

Some of the more lucid patients in the unit were frustrated, sharing with me how they were blatantly ignored no matter if what they revealed to the staff were imperative needs or intimate thoughts. A theme I heard from many was if they showed emotion the response was to have a pill shoved down their throat.

Most of them clearly appreciated someone taking the time to sit and listen to them. Were they "playing me, the fool"? I was warned of this and did not have enough experience with psych patients to figure it out myself, at least not this early in my residency. I harkened back to the days I spoke about in my introduction, the days in the pool-hall; the days where I learned about looking at telling signs of what's happening by observing body language

I proceeded with my daily activities, opening my heart and trusting my judgment, investing fully in all aspects of this rigorous residency. If I were being "played the fool," I would learn from the experience, and if the concerns of the patients were real, hopefully I could offer some spiritual solace and much-needed compassion. I did not see the staff or patients as "enemy." I saw them both as complex beings, each with a unique history, all ultimately from a Divine Source. I refused to stereotype either group, committed to remaining opened.

After several weeks of reliably progressing in this way, the staff realized I was not a threat. As such, they requested I visit a man, Herman, who had refused to come out of his room for weeks. Entering the room I saw a man, in his mid-seventies, staring blankly into space. I introduced myself, however he did not respond. I sat with him in silence hoping he might acknowledge me. He did not and after a period of time, I left the room.

The next day I returned to him in his room, to the same silent response. Our routine went on for a few days. The staff informed me that he was scheduled for electric shock therapy the next day. He was being prepared. The team, with permission of family, said this would be the only way to get a response. It was at this point I learned his wife of fifty-five years had died and since that time he had become unresponsive, almost catatonic. People respond to loss differently. This patient could not conceive that his wife had left the world. He was in his own world of grief and couldn't imagine where she was. If he left his room, he felt he would not be able to ever find her again. Each time I passed the room, he would go to the door and look around, however he would not leave his space of silence or step over the threshold into the hallway.

The thought of electric shock appalled me and I perceived it as abuse. I would make another attempt. I entered the room and sat down next to him. I pleaded, "Please talk to me, Herman! Tell me the thoughts from your heart." He said, "I miss Ida! I miss Ida!" And, after exclaiming this twice, he said nothing more. Now I understood the depth of his all-consuming grief. I sat with him and held his hand. I knew he was feeling as his eyes were full of tears. Taking a deep breath, I made myself comfortable, readying myself to stay here for as long as would be necessary given the development, and began surveying the room.

The walls were barren, though the drab green paint stood out. This heaviness was enough to depress even the most joyful of individuals. My thoughts turned to my home where I am surrounded, by not only art, but by pictures of me and my wife together, our children, and our grandchildren. I know knew this was all cut off from Herman. His memories were nowhere to be found – they disappeared, leaving only the heavy lethargy of a depressed patient. The room was void of life force. Herman had some personal belongings, though not enough to really make much of an impression in the immediate environs. I left the room, and as I passed the nurse's station I noticed the doctor was present. I requested a brief audience and it was granted.

"I know you are planning to shock Herman tomorrow. Is this really necessary?"

The doctor was extremely defensive, "We do it all the time. Besides, the family gave permission."

I asked rhetorically, then speaking fast enough that I may complete my request, though all the while choosing my words extremely carefully, "May I make a suggestion? After Herman's wife died he was not able to cope and went into this deep depression. He sat *shiva* (the seven day period of mourning) with his family and then was placed in this facility. I believe he has not been given the space to properly grieve."

"I would like to contact his children and have them bring pictures of Herman and Ida to the hospital. I then propose we hang some of these images and sit with Herman and attempt to have him speak to me about their lives together. Would you consider postponing the shock treatment for a few days and see if I am able to make headway? Please let the man grieve."

The doctor simply quipped, "I'll think about it," and dismissed me.

I left the unit not knowing if my request would be granted so, the next day I arrived early so I could be with Herman prior to his scheduled treatment. I found that the procedure had been canceled for the day! I was told his children were coming to visit later and, in fact, they would be bringing photographs with them. I was overjoyed and deeply relieved my proposal had been accepted. The doctor even gave orders to hang the pictures throughout the room. The nurse, unbeknownst to her how these events had developed, was clearly intrigued with the doctor's unique therapy for Herman.

The next day, as I walked into the room, Herman greeted me and invited me to sit with him. His presence was radically transformed. The room was full of pictures of him and Ida. He pulled out additional picture books and as we reviewed each picture he explained where he and Ida were and what they had been doing. Every few moments a tear would come to his eye. He was finally able to cry. After encouraging him to allow the tears to come, he cried even more, the catharsis palpable. The renewed family visits continued over a period of three days, each day revealing a newly animated Herman. I was off for the weekend and assured Herman I would visit with him first thing on Monday.

Arriving Monday morning as promised, and expecting to find Herman in his room, much to my surprise, instead I found another patient present. Herman had, in fact, been released and returned home, rehabilitated and able to be on his own once again. Herman had not needed electric shock therapy after all. What he clearly needed was compassion, love, understanding and the time to appropriately grieve his beloved.

Several weeks passed. The doctor neglected to acknowledge my suggestion for helping Herman directly. He did, however, include me in the rounds, occasionally request my input and even sought my consult regarding certain other more significant cases. I knew and the doctor knew, even though he had not as yet acknowledged it, that I had helped Herman recover. This event enabled me to trust my intuition when an answer is not evident. Together, the doctor and I now forming more of a partnership in this unit, were able to confer with many other patients and families offering more thorough and diverse treatment options.

All the while I was investing in my work as a resident, I knew when my rotation was concluded, I would not be allowed back on the unit. This was the rule. No chaplains were allowed to simply "drop by" for a visit. All staff presences had to be requested, through official channels. Upon leaving, however, I was told that the doctor had written an addendum officially declaring I was welcome on the unit at any time, even without the previously required official invitation. In time, this invitation was extended to other certified chaplains.

As our loved ones age and decline and we watch that decline, how do we behave and react? Some of us care for them, nurture them and try our best to understand what's happening in their heads. Others are unable cope with the loss of their parents being "present" because they are unable to face it out of sadness and longing for the "old days". Some, unfortunately, simply do not care. This brings me to a time when Jackie's mother was in hospice, suffering from dementia and close to leaving the world. My mother-in-law called Jackie and told her that she must come and visit right away, as her parents (Jackie's long dead grandparents), were coming to have lunch with her and wanted to see Jackie. Jackie reminded her that they died in 1956, but that didn't deter my mother-in-law, or Jackie. She ran right over to have lunch with her Mom, and of course, her Mom asked Jackie why she was there. By this time she had completely forgotten about the phone call. So, as an adult child of a parent who is declining, what is our responsibility? Jackie answered the call to honor her mother, and her grandparents, who were probably calling from another world. But, how many of us ignore the call and just chalk it up to dementia.

Electric shock therapy continues to be practiced in this renowned institution, but hopefully they are no longer using such intensive treatments until other means of healing are explored.

*   *   *

My parents, also, suffered a painful decline, not necessarily due to mental illness, but another kind of illness that is rampant among the senior community. My parents, of blessed memory, were both addicted to prescription medications. My father's death certificate reads that he died from a heart attack; such is the claim. However, he was visiting five different doctors and three different dentists, all prescribing to him quite powerful medications. As soon as Jackie and I became aware this was happening we immediately confronted these doctors. Ultimately, we were told to mind our own business. Then, taking matters further into my own hands longing to remedy this unnecessary plight, I confronted my father about his addiction and offered to support him in a treatment facility. His only response was that he did not speak to me for a year. Even after this devastating year of silence, afterwards he would only entertain casual conversation with me.

Following his death, I moved my mother to Minnesota to live near me. At this time, she was also visibly near death. A friend of mine at the time was a local physician and, upon her arrival and surveying her state, he took her off all unnecessary medications. He proved to be extremely thorough and patient, making the time to analyze the necessary medications for her continued health, removing all others from her treatment. She lived a quality life for ten years.

At the time of my father's death, Jackie immediately threw his pills down the toilet. I do not have an accurate count of the pills, however I would say the illegal street value was worth lots of money. My parents lived in a retirement community. The people who lived in the community were angry with my wife and confronted her. They said the pills were promised to them and there was an unwritten agreement that whenever a community member died, their pills would be distributed. This was a big issue as so many people in this community were, in fact, addicted to prescription pain killers --- and because the addiction was so strong, they oftentimes ran out of meds before they could be refilled. The fear of running out of pills overtook their lives to the point where they would seek out drugs wherever they could find them, legally or not. Overdosing our seniors to keep them quiet is tragically common in our society today.

Where is our responsibility to our seniors? We are allowing them to be over medicated and we feel secure if they just stay quiet. We must teach them to live fully and die well. It's as if we're trying to blot out the past in order to not have to face our own certain future, namely the unavoidable aging process. We must respect and learn from our elders, sharing their unique lessons with the following generations.

Judaism has the high commandment of *L'dor v'dor* (lit., "from generation to generation"). We take the stories, wisdom, life lessons and more from our ancestors, expand upon them and go forward so we may leave them as an inheritance to our children, grandchildren and great grandchildren, etc. The skills of our seniors and the life-adventures they have lived are, truly, priceless. Now, however, we turn to our computer for *information* as opposed to the *wisdom* we have available to us. We must learn to sit and listen, once again, to our elders, not only for information, but also for their accumulated wisdom.

The Survivor

I OFFICIATE AT MANY FUNERALS. Because I work as a hospice Chaplain, this responsibility and honor is inevitable. If I haven't had the opportunity to personally get to know the deceased, I speak with family members who tell me stories, show me pictures and invite me into the lives of their loved ones. After I meet with these folks, I meditate in order to get acquainted with the deceased so I can lift them up and honor them at the same time.

I AM FREQUENTLY ASKED TO OFFICIATE AT FUNERALS. Sometimes I know the family quite well, and other times I have met them only once or twice, sometimes not at all. I was to officiate at the funeral of an elderly woman that I did not know. The funeral director requested that I officiate because this funeral service was a special case, one that would require compassion, patience and understanding. First, I met with the woman's husband prior to the service to find out some facts about his wife, himself, their relationship and their family.

Max, the husband, was a short man standing just over five feet. He had a round face, soft bulging cheeks that met his eyes. His white beard hid his many chins. His eyes were red from crying and his aged-spotted hands were trembling. He began by sharing with me that he and his wife, Sadie, met before the war. And, in his deep Polish accent, he told me his story…

"We were teenagers, but I knew immediately she was my *basheret*. It was hard, those days in Poland. I saw families being persecuted and my friends were 'disappearing' all the time --- day and night we lived in terror. I knew times would get better and this was temporary, but when?

Life went on. I don't have to tell you, things got worse. A lot worse. The Nazis were in control and they had a mission to wipe us out." He began to weep and, through his tears, he continued sharing with me.

"I was a young man when our door was broken down. They stormed our house, stealing all of my parent's possessions before they burned our home. We watched in disbelief and horror as our home turned into the funeral pyre of the life we knew. We were lined up with our neighbors --- my mother, father, two sisters, grandmother and myself. We stood in a straight line, as ordered. I glanced across the road and noticed my Sadie, my *basheret*, standing with her family on the other side of the road. Our eyes met and, instead of observing these murderers, we gazed at each other."

"Having completed their destruction of our homes and places of sanctuary, they went down the row inspecting each of us, one-by-one. I was ordered to stand to one side. I obeyed. I saw across the road that my Sadie was also on this side. Separated into two rows now, those on the opposite side of Sadie and I were ordered to walk into a large crater that had been dug a few kilometers down the road. The rest of us remained in our assigned spot. From the distance I heard the piercing blasts of machine gun fire. People were screaming with pain and terror. And then, nothing, but the sound of bulldozers as the crater was filled.

My family, my neighbors and my friends were now dead, their bodies buried as quickly as the flight of their souls. I was filled with terror, fear and rage as the solders returned telling jokes and laughing. I, along with the others in my line, was placed on a truck and taken to a work camp. It was filthy and smelled of death. The rats ran freely and we were tattooed, branded like cattle." He rolled up his sleeve revealing the faded numbers forever stained into his arm.

"We were stripped of our clothes and, along with them, our dignity, dirty prison clothes thrown at us to wear. A few people complained, or asked a question and were shot and killed in response. I kept my mouth shut, though I was screaming inside. My mind quickly escaped to other regions, where I was with my family and with my Sadie. I wondered constantly whether or not any of them were still alive.

Torture and death became as common as breathing. When a person died we scurried to remove their shoes, thinking maybe they had less holes than ours, along with any other possessions that may prove functional or valuable enough to barter with. Our interest was living only for the next day in the hope that release from hell would come. During this time I had become reduced to an animal-state, scavenging for sustenance. Hate for our torturers kept me going from one day to the next. At this point, I *knew* there was no God!"

"One day, after about a year and a half, I walked from the tiny barracks and found the camp deserted. What was happening? I heard trucks and hid. When I dared to peek I saw American soldiers. We were liberated! I was taken to a hospital. I was fed and my decayed body was mended. My teeth were pulled because they could not be saved and I was given false teeth. The tattoo remained on my arm, and the vision of my family being murdered remained on my soul."

"I returned to my village in Poland to find destruction --- *total* destruction. Rabbi," Max confided, "it was terrible…nearly unrecognizable. All the beauty was gone. Upon my return I met others who had also wandered from place to place in an attempt to rebuild what was once their home. I stayed for a, while attempting to find my Sadie, though no matter how hard I try to search for my buried treasure, so to speak, I did not find her. I walked to the crater to visit where my family had been exterminated and buried. Grass had grown over the pit and weeds had taken over the site."

Eventually I was able gain passage on a ship bound for America, thus I promptly left Europe. The ship was crowded and quarters were tight, but nothing compared to the terrors I had so recently survived. I slept on the deck where there was a bit more space and, at least, fresh air. Needless to say, this was a great improvement from the death camp.

We floated in to New York and passed the Statue of Liberty. Goose bumps, tears of joy and hope filled me upon the site of her fabled shore. 'A new life!,' I exclaimed. While being processed on Ellis Island, I looked around at the thousands and thousands of people. And now, before my very eyes, I saw the most beautiful sight in the world: My Sadie! My *basheret*! She was there --- *here* --- she was alive! I ran to her and we embraced and have never parted, until now"

"So, Rabbi, I have to tell you, nobody ever recited *Kaddish* for my family and, up to this time, I did not want to recite *any* prayers. My soul had grown hardened." Tears were streaming down his face. "Would it be all right for me to recite the *Kaddish* at Sadie's grave?" I encouraged him to do so.

Many of the people I visit and get to know in hospice have blue numbers tattooed on their fore arms revealing immediately that they are a holocaust survivor. Some of them will talk about their lives in the camps, their loss of family and loved ones and some, still, are not able to do so. I have noticed there is a gap between their practice and belief in God and their abandonment of any God-space in their lives. I do not "over-God" them. I do not directly react to their thinking, as at this time in their lives, it is not my place to "fix" or "heal" them. When Max revealed that he had never recited *Kaddish* for any of his family members I knew that any connection to God that he might have had, had faded away. Knowing this, the revelation of him requesting to recite *Kaddish* for his wife and relatives, who were long ago murdered, was overwhelming and significant.

Family, friends, neighbors and acquaintances attended the service at the synagogue. I was profoundly moved as I blessed his children, grandchildren and great-grandchildren with the blessing of *l'dor v'dor*, that they should remember their *Bubbie*, teach her lessons and tell her stories to their children, grandchildren and great-grandchildren to keep her memory alive as an inherited yet living treasure. Indeed, I shared with them doing so enables her to live through them for many generations and fulfills the *mitzvah* of *l'dor v'dor*. I recited "*El molay Rachamim*," and we proceeded to the grave. The coffin was lowered as I recited Psalms. I then told those gathered that Sadie had been present throughout the entire service. "She is not here to hear *my* words," I assured them, "but to join with all of you, each of you, in your heart." I continued to tell them that as the coffin is covered with earth, her soul will be released, free to complete its ultimate mission.

I then requested Max to lead us through the recitation of *Kaddish*.

"*Yis-gad-dal v'yis-kad-dash sh'mey rab-bo…*"

Max's voice pierced the hearts of all present, reaching heavenward to those who had passed from his world. As he annunciated each word, I had the palpable sense angels were surrounding the entire cemetery. Max's trembling, heart-full voice sounded radiant and full, like blasts from a *shofar*. Through his recitation he opened the gates for all the lost souls, all those murdered with the words *Shema Yisrael* on their lips during their last seconds of life. Tears came to my eyes and my body trembled as we recited, "*Kadosh, Kadosh, Kadosh* --- all is Holy…"

At the end of a funeral service, people are asked to rise and recite *Kaddish* for their loved ones who have recently passed. I choose to stand and recite Kaddish for all those who have no one to say *Kaddish* for them. My teacher, Reb David Wolf Blank, *z'l*, taught me that each time one recites *Kaddish* sparks of energy are sent to the soul of the person for whom we are reciting this prayer. My hope is to raise and energize six million sparks of energy in my lifetime.

Beauty Beneath The Surface

I am my beloved, and my beloved is mine.

- Song of Songs, 6:3-13

I HAVE MET AND LISTENED to the stories of many women and their families whose lives have been overtaken with the challenges of breast cancer. It is an epidemic. Some of the women I have been with have been newly diagnosed and have undergone a lumpectomy, followed by chemotherapy and/or radiation. Some have had radical mastectomies, followed by reconstructive surgery. Some have had elective mastectomies because they have a genetic breast cancer probability. All of these women are forced to wrestle with their emotions as their lives continue. The overwhelming emotion is the fear of an early death due to the cancer metastasizing. Some who have had mastectomies are in fear because their appearance has been changed. I have had meetings and conversations with physicians who reconstruct the breast following a mastectomy as well as tattoo artists who specialize in creating the natural look of a breast following reconstruction surgery. Most of the women who have gone through this are fine with their appearance, but confide in me that they no longer have any feeling in their breasts. Even with successful reconstructive surgery, many of the women feel they have suffered a permanent loss of their value as a complete woman.

WHEN I AM SCHEDULED TO BE THE CHAPLAIN ON-CALL, an undisturbed night of sleep becomes a blessing. My alarm clock, usually a routine annoyance, transforms into a sweet melody, precious as it wakes me in the morning in contrast with the pager, which signals an emergency. Usually during these on-call nights, however, the pager alerts me to an emergency, often times an accident or even a death.

On this particular night it was roughly 3 a.m. when I heard the dreaded pager begin to whine. I stumbled to the phone to triage the call when I was instructed to come to the hospital immediately. It sounded as if a woman was crying incessantly and could not be calmed by the staff, though the details remained largely unknown to me at this point. I took a quick shower to waken and refresh myself, wondering about the details, "why did I get called in the middle of the night for a woman crying? Why couldn't the staff control such a situation? Surely there is more transpiring…"

I arrived at the hospital and quickly navigated to the assigned floor. I learned that the woman was in a private room and, prior to entering, I took the necessary time to review her chart. Wendy was a 29-year-old woman who had a radical mastectomy earlier in the day. I entered, and saw Wendy, a beautiful woman, sitting on the side of the bed. Her red eyes and cheeks spoke stories of loss, fear and great sadness. Her long brown hair was disheveled, flattened from the time spent in recovery, lying on her pillow, soaked by tears. The blue hospital gown she wore was spotted and wrinkled. A picture of two small children in the protective arms of a smiling man stood on the table. I assumed this was her family.

I introduced myself. She looked at me through her tears and thanked me for coming. I took her hand and held it as I asked her to tell me why she was upset. I knew about the mastectomy; however I wanted to hear her speak in her own words in order to analyze her story so I could join in and share the burden of her fear and grief. Although I read the patient's charts prior to my visit, I always ask the patient to tell me what happened to them so I can relate to them and offer them the opportunity to externalize their hidden feelings, whatever they may be.

She said, "I found a small lump on my breast, so I went to the doctor. He sent me for a mammogram and an ultra sound. He said that the lump would have to be removed, and that it was a simple procedure: They would put me to sleep, remove the lump, and send me home when I woke up. They said if the lump contains cancer cells, I might have to have some radiation therapy when I healed. I woke up in the recovery room and the doctor was standing over me. He said the cancer in my breast was worse than anticipated --- it was very aggressive. In order for it not to spread, he had to remove my breast. He told me that although I would receive either radiation or chemotherapy, he was able to remove the entire tumor and my outlook was favorable for a full recovery. He told me I was very lucky." The words very and lucky rolled out of her mouth like lead. She looked at me through her tears and asked, "Do I look like I was very lucky?"

I did not answer --- there are times when even our words of support are not enough --- giving her the space to proceed. She spoke about preparing for the operation and the devastating shock upon waking to this unexpected reality. She spoke in an anxious, urgent tone, without a pause, for about 15 minutes, as if speaking faster and faster could aid her in sprinting past time and into the past where she might reclaim part of her body, now removed. I sat with Wendy, listening and feeling deeply for this young woman. When she had exhausted herself --- remember, she's just beginning the recovery process from a mastectomy earlier in the day --- she looked directly at me. I asked her to continue and upon hearing these words she broke down and sunk into my arms. As I held her she said, "I am a young woman, and my husband --- that's him in the picture with my children --- is a handsome man. We take pride in our appearance. We work out, watch our diet, and are known to our friends as, 'the striking couple.' Do you really think he will want to be with me? Do you think he will want to make love to me, a freak with one breast? How can I still be desirable as a woman? All I have are stiches and scars. I look like Frankenstein! They tell me I can have reconstruction surgery in a happy tone. Do they think that makes me happy?"

Wendy continued to sob and, while heartbreaking, I recognized as she vented her anger and released these pent-up emotions she was engaging an immensely crucial process. My job now was simply to remain present and compassionate, supporting her and facilitating her emotional recovery in any way my position allowed for. I asked her if she had spoken to her husband after the surgery. She said he was there, and that he hugged and kissed her and told her that he loves her.

"He hasn't seen my chest!" She declared in a loud screaming voice. "I have one breast and a bandage for the other."

At this point I could have attempted to reassure her about her inner beauty, the beauty of her children and how the inner self is stronger than the outer manifestation. I could have spoken to her about reconstructive surgery. I felt the clear instruction to abstain from any of those particular pathways, however. Instead, I stayed with her holding her until she cried herself to sleep and then I left the room.

Sometimes our words are not enough, hollow in the face of significant loss, and during these times we must permit people to grieve without interference. I think of the Jewish tradition: when entering a house of mourning we do not approach the mourners, or even address them, for that matter. Instead, we wait, offer our presence and positive energy --- ultimately, we offer our complete love --- not speaking until we are invited to by those suffering. This situation was no different. She was mourning a loss and I was her visitor. I stayed with her at bedside until she fell asleep close to dawn.

It was morning and the sun was rising. I decided to stay at the hospital. I took a catnap on the sofa in the on-call room, the room designated for professionals such as chaplains and other such staff, and waited to meet Wendy's husband when he came to visit. I awoke to the floor nurse informing me Wendy's husband had arrived.

I went to the room and stood by the door, remaining a passive witness as Wendy and her husband embraced. The drabness of her room I noticed only a few hours ago had seemingly disappeared as the room was now filled with, bright flowers and sunshine. Re-entering, I introduced myself to Ed, Wendy's husband. Wendy remembered me, even through the cloud of pain medication she must have been in when we first spoke, and thanked me for staying with her last night. I sat down with them, and asked if I could share a lesson from a story from my rabbi and teacher, Reb Shlomo Carlebach, z'l.

The story is about how we see each other. When we look at each other with good eyes, we see into the soul of the person we are with. What are good eyes? They are the eyes that do not judge who we are or what we may look like on the surface. They are the eyes of that which is in the deepest part of our soul --- where all of the beauty in the Universe comes from. When we see each other with good eyes we see from our heart, and we then have the ability to heal ourselves, others and even the entire Universe.

"So, dearest Wendy and Ed, I bless you to be able to always look at each other with good eyes, to witness each other as individuals and together as a couple. I bless you to see your beautiful children under the wedding canopy and I bless you with peace and healing."

I knew I could not really know how their relationship would mature. However, I was sure that if they see each other with "good eyes," they would be able to have open hearts for one another. If they are able to maintain this space and such a connection, they will have the inner strength to travel the road of life, exploring all of its ups and downs together. They would not only find the heart of their own souls --- and, in so doing, that of the other --- they would be able to feel through to the Heart and Soul of our Universe, one of the threads that unites us all. The path was opened for them to relate to this major event as a blessing. It was this landscape of possibility I saw for them as I blessed them.

Wendy had suffered a terrible loss and she was grieving. We lose jobs, income, health and ability to discern. We lose people to death whom we love. At times, we even lose love. We grieve losses in different ways as they touch different parts of our personalities, where we see ourselves as now in contrast with who it is we strive to become as our lives unfold.

Wendy needed the space to grieve and accept her loss in her own way and her own time. If not given this space I believe her grief would dominate her life and distract from the pleasure she would receive as a wife, mother and woman. She was fortunate that her husband was supportive.

The witnessing of the interaction of Wendy and Ed's emotional landscape enabled me to recognize how beauty resides beneath the surface if one is viewed with "good eyes". This is not a tale about the medical procedures for the treatment of breast cancer. This story is about sensitivity and support for any woman facing such a loss. This encounter also deepened my awareness about the epidemic of breast cancer and that from that time forward, I have personally encouraged all women to receive annual check-ups, to perform regular personal breast checks, and to get a mammogram so that if breast cancer does emerge, it is detected early and treated properly.

The Wedding Canopy

GRIEF IS ONE OF THE MOST OVERWHELMING emotions that keep us paralyzed from moving forward in our lives. People ask me about the length of time they should grieve and when these feelings of powerlessness will cease. Unfortunately, I have to tell them that it will never be over, however, they will find the strength to move on with their lives.

A personal story: Our children were visiting from out of town and they wanted Jackie to cook a brisket, something she hadn't prepared for many years. We went to the butcher and ordered a beautiful trimmed brisket for the evening meal. At the counter, she said to me that she had forgotten how to cook the perfect brisket. Without thinking, I said to Jackie, "call Mom." Now, my mother had left the world five years earlier. At that moment, grief visited us and tears flowed, first from missing my mother, and then we laughed with tears, remembering how much she would have enjoyed the moment --- as well as a delicious brisket. So when it comes to grief, and the timing of grieving, my response always is "listen to your heart."

I FACILITATE MANY GRIEF GROUPS. These groups are open to anyone who has suffered a loss, no matter the specifics. I do not judge why they attend as anyone who is in a state of grief has suffered a loss, their hearts and lives shattered in some way, to whatever degree. My groups are interdenominational and multicultural. Usually the attendees have suffered a loss from death of a loved one, however I also welcome participants who have suffered the loss of a job, home, particular lifestyle or a pet as just some examples. My grief groups have very few formal requirements partly inspired by the fact that I recognize grief is cruel and has no boundaries itself --- sometimes we have to deal with this unruly shadow in unlimited ways. It can make known its unwelcomed presence at any time and, as we may fall into its clutches, we seem to sustain its momentum as it becomes more powerful over our emotions and states of being.

Some facilitators have suggested I run a more formal, "traditional" grief group with rules, where participants must sign a legal waiver to attend. In my experience, it's these very facilitators that eventually find themselves sitting in an empty room waiting for participants to show up for a "formal" meeting. Grief and its related support groups do not always benefit as much from such sterile environments, but need more breathing room, so to speak. My perspective and applied theoretical approach does not threaten or turn a person away, but embraces their needs in a gentle understanding manner, inviting them to attend fully, whoever and *however* they may be.

Once a woman attended one of my groups who was very confused by the loss of her mother to cancer a month prior. She had been very close with her mother who was, indeed, her best friend. She shared her intimate thoughts and emotions with the group now assembled. "We shopped together. We laughed and cried together. We loved each other immeasurably. I miss her so much! We spoke every day. I now look at the front door, but she doesn't appear; she no longer calls me on the phone."

The group remained silent after she shared. Eventually I addressed how lucky she was to be able to feel and share in such a way about her mother. The group collectively began to share, each individual contributing in depth, regarding the power of relationships with our parents and siblings. It led to tears of joy, tears of anger for those who did not have a good relationship with their parent, even tears of envy. It was a good session. We were able to welcome clarity and understanding. I could not "fix" the participant's problems, feelings or issues. Indeed, that is not my training, nor my desire. However they had some thoughts to embrace and hopefully think about. They spoke to each other and shared their stories. I always begin a group by stating if someone wishes to share they are welcome. My task is to jump in only for clarity or to keep someone from dominating the group.

The woman who spoke of her mother remained. Her eyes filled with tears as she began sharing more with me in private after the group had been dismissed.

"My daughter is getting married in five weeks. We have a huge wedding planned and all the details are now set. Should I cancel the wedding or go on in the face of this loss? My daughter and her wonderful fiancée said it is my decision." I reflected the question back to her and asked what she wished to do.

"I really would like the wedding to proceed," she stated. "However I feel guilty planning to celebrate anything during this time, with how I'm feeling since my mother's passing." We spoke about guilt and betrayal within the grief process.

I paused and thought of how we allow our lives to be controlled by guilt. The guilt may stem from sources related to our family or from the greater society we are born into, and sometimes we allow it to dictate our feelings, we even allow it to engulf us and exert dominion over us. We sometimes unnecessarily take on this guilt and in such times it affects not only us, but also all of the people we come in contact with. It manifests to the point of sometimes rendering us physically ill and socially impotent. We joke about Jewish guilt and Catholic guilt, etc. All the religions, ethnicities and cultures have guilt as a psychological challenge at the top of their list. It is time to realize we are energizing this guilt. It has no power of it's own, and we not only can, but must stop it! Living with guilt at the front of our consciousness engulfs our everyday life and dictates our behavior and activities because it makes opaque our truths and free choice. Guilt does not allow us to make clear decisions --- instead it muddles our awareness and blocks connection to our true self.

"Obviously, I cannot advise you whether to proceed with the wedding or postpone it for now. It has to be your decision." But, I inquired into a few details I was intuiting might have greater significance, should the wedding take place as scheduled. I asked her if her daughter was planning to be married under a *chupah* (the traditional "wedding canopy" the bride and groom stand under during the wedding ceremony). She replied, in fact, they were planning to be married under the *chupah*.

"You know, when the rabbi, bride and groom stand under the *chupah* during a wedding ceremony, they are joined by a myriad of visitors from the beyond. All the angels, in fact, join in with them, as do the souls of all the relatives who have previously left the world, all showering blessings on them. Your mother will be under the *chupah* with your daughter. She will bless your daughter." The woman smiled, thanked me and left.

After about two months she appeared at group and was glowing with clearly renewed energy since we first met. She came to share with the group about the wedding ceremony. She spoke how she felt not only her mother's presence, but also poignantly sensing the presence of other relatives who had previously left our world. She said she felt in her heart that the angels and lost family members were present and blessing the union. As she continued with details of the happy union her tears flowed, as did those of the rest of us gathered at this meeting. I smiled knowing that the group had to hear this account for it was an inspiring and heart-warming update. A fundamental technique of group therapy and healing is asking for individuals to tell their story, because whatever they are going through, have gone through, or will go through, someone else has likely had a similar experience and might be able to convey their feelings. In our spiritual practices we share and enhance the stories of our matriarchs, patriarchs and prophets. We can be each other's guides as we share and listen to one another.

I ended the group early that evening. I had an engagement for which I could not be late. Leaving, I felt a bit guilty for ending early, however I was able to hear my own words about guilt and embrace my feelings. I had a great evening.

Part of my morning routine is setting aside time for prayer and meditation. Some mornings I am able to take this precious time, read and learn from holy books and some mornings I am rushed. On the mornings I am rushed I close my eyes and I say, *"Ribono Shel Olam* --- 'Master of the Universe,' You know what's deep inside me…untie the tangles for me and my loved ones." Do I feel guilty that I did not read all the texts, dotting the I's and crossing the T's, so to speak? No, I do not. I feel I have made a direct connection with the Holy One and we shared time and space together, and it is this intimacy that truly matters.

Section II.

Helping Release Blockage

I BELIEVE THAT *MEDITATION* can sometimes be more effective than *medication* for clearing the spaces that are blocking our thoughts and actions. I say this because in my work, I've oftentimes seen the effect of over medication and how it masks problems instead of allowing patients to deal with their problems, I believe that meditation, in fact, helps to clear the mind so people can connect to the root of their soul and move forward in their lives. I speak as a Chaplain, not a medical doctor, psychiatrist or psychologist and encourage those individuals who require cognitive and emotional support to engage those powerful allies and remedies, if necessary. I was visiting a patient suffering with COPD (chronic obstructive pulmonary disease). He was talking about an event that occurred with his son where there was a disagreement on the patient's part. As he went on with the story he became more and more upset and started to flair his arms in the air. He soon started gasping for breath. He reached for his inhaler, which offered only minimal relief. I sat next to him and encouraged him to breathe slowly with me and visualize calm, calm, calm. Soon his breathing became less and less labored and we were able to continue our visit.

The literal meaning of the Hebrew word, *k'lipah*, is "husk," as an outer covering, or shell. In the mystical schools of Judaism we learn that it is a *k'lipah* that, until transformed, blocks our heart and soul, not allowing us to grow, evolve and transform our lives. It is taught that even if we use the might of a sledgehammer to try and break through this covering, it will have no effect. However, if we address this shell covering and insulating our heart from the inside-out, with nothing but the effort of a light feather we can shatter the husk.

The stories I share below demonstrate how we are most effectively able to break through the blockages in our bodies and minds, with understanding and compassion, helping them to be released and, thus, liberating an undue, self-inflicted and self-managed emotional and psychological pain.

Holy Bagpipes

WE ALL USE TOOLS in our daily lives. The painter uses a brush, the carpenter a hammer and we are all increasingly dependent upon computers and cell phones. Our tools of prayer are different depending upon beliefs and religions. Our prayer, however, is going to the same source, although each prayer may travel via different routes, according to one's tradition. My road of prayer is via the Torah and Her teachings. The following story demonstrates how the Torah scroll was significant in the healing of a family, while at the same time, was seen by someone who knew nothing about this holy scroll and visualized it according to her cultural and spiritual beliefs.

THE SNOW WAS MELTING IN MINNESOTA, and spring was beginning to thaw the frigid darkness of winter: though the snow on the roads lingered and had turned black from the traffic, the birds were chirping, calling-in for the coming season of light and renewal. The entrance of the hospital had a clear walkway, surrounded by mountains of decaying snow making for a noticeably chilling entrance to an institution that has come to symbolize a place of "winter" for so many of us.

My first visit of the day was to the oncology unit. This unit's staff has a very difficult task. They provide presence to people who are dying and witness the patients' bodies deteriorating on a daily basis. They become close to the patients and caregivers. And, though they may cry on the inside, on the outside, however, they are professional and present, offering constant compassion and understanding in awe-inspiringly consistent and angelic ways.

I was requested to see a Jewish patient in room number 408. Upon entering the room, I was warmly greeted by a man in his early seventies; his name was Ralph.

Ralph was clean-shaven and his thick graying hair neatly combed. His eyes were open wide, bright with hope and yet also searching, as if for something lost. His wife of 40 years, Shirley, was also present in the room, her attire reflected the Minnesota season. She was well kempt wearing a combination of bright and subdued clothes. Her winter weight olive colored sweater and slacks were brightened by colorful scarves and jewelry.

Ralph, after numerous tests, had recently received a diagnosis of stomach cancer. We spoke at length about their feelings about this diagnosis as well as towards the cancer itself, as a presence. Ralph and Shirley recalled how they had been through many challenges in life thus far, and this was only another. They were determined Ralph was going to best even this new, acute trial.

I allowed them the space to communicate their feelings with me as well as witnessing them sharing and connecting with one another. They spoke about their family --- two sons and four grandchildren --- with pride. They shared with me about their business and how delightful retirement had been for the past few years. Ralph, embodying a sort of prototypical American spirit, did not consider himself a religious man, though he considered himself to be very active spiritually. He had explored Eastern religions and, through such explorations, had developed his own way of reaching out to God, developing his own meditations and prayers that most directly spoke the language of his heart. These meditations and prayers came from a pure heart-place, clearly symbolic of his love for God.

Ralph knew his health was declining and I had been trained to know that anger is present during this deterioration process. I subsequently addressed the issue of anger toward the diagnosis. He said, "Hell yes, I have a lot of anger. I also have a hell of a lot more living to do." I admired his down-to-earth attitude.

The surgeon was to operate on Ralph later in the day, thus they requested I offer a traditional healing prayer for him as he settled down to rest.

"Master of the Universe, God of our ancestors", I stand here with Ralph, who is about to undergo surgery. Please guide the surgeon's hands as he operates on Ralph. Let this surgeon be mindful of his task and give him the fortitude and skill to completely remove the cancer from Ralph."

"Let Ralph's body welcome the procedure, and send your angel Rafael to join with him, strengthening his body and soul. Please capture all the cancer cells, and grant him a healing of body, mind and spirit."

"Let the love that Ralph and Shirley share for one another energize their souls, bringing them ever closer to you and to each other. Amen."

I hugged both Ralph and Shirley before leaving the room. I checked in on Ralph, once in recovery, and he was doing well. The doctor reported he was able to remove most of the cancer and Ralph would receive chemotherapy and radiation in the coming months in an attempt to irradiate the remaining cells. Ralph received his treatments as prescribed. At this point he was treated through outpatient care and would travel to the hospital three days each week for his chemotherapy treatment. During this phase of his treatment I would visit Ralph at his home.

I can compare his appearance to the passing seasons in Minnesota. As the fall and winter came, the weather turned dark and gloomy. The bitter cold pierced not only one's skin, but shook one's soul . Ralph's appearance reflected much of the cold barrenness in the surrounding landscape: his hair was falling out more rapidly than even the leaves on the frozen trees. His face was pale, white and grey as the snow outside, eyes dark and hollow, revealing his once filled out cheekbones, now sunken as the near barren trees outside his window.

I thought of the bare branches of the trees, standing alone and naked. I wanted to tell him that new leaves would come in the spring, that his body and soul would only grow stronger and bear ripe fruit, however I knew it was not to be. After consulting with the physicians and nurses assigned to his case, I knew that Ralph's prognoses was grim and his chances of surviving this cancer minimal, if not impossible. His once-strong body shivered as he wrapped himself in his blanket. His voice was faint like the barely noticeable movement of winter across the sky. As I placed my ear close to his face, his diminished and muffled words struggled to be heard.

Ralph was losing his battle. I would visit him about once a month and each time I saw him he'd become noticeably weaker. And yet, he always remained cordial, ready for my visit and welcoming me in as an intimate friend. Shirley would make us lunch and have Jewish klezmer music playing on the stereo, which lightened the scene.

It was during these scheduled visits with Ralph that we came to the point in our relationship where Ralph was ready to speak directly about mortality. Whenever I engage with a patient close to death, it ultimately makes me face my own death and therefore, I felt that Ralph and I were facing death together as we spoke about the soul and where it may travel after it leaves the body. We talked about life and, I reminded Ralph, although he felt worn out, he was currently one hundred percent alive! I encouraged him to live each second to the fullest. He spoke of his family, of not being able to see his grandchildren under the *chupah* as their wedding celebration was about to take place. I assured him that he would be there in spirit to offer his blessings. I had many visits with Ralph and Shirley that winter.

Winter ultimately transformed to spring and once again the birds were chirping, however Ralph could not hear them: he was back in the hospital, comatose. It appeared the time for his soul to leave his body was drawing closer. I visited daily, directing my support and compassion to Shirley, his sons and the rest of the hospital staff members that had become close to Ralph and his family.

The days passed and turned to weeks, Ralph still residing between the state of life and death. I knew, from past experience, sometimes a person will refuse to leave our world if they feel they have unfinished business. I sat with Shirley and on one occasion she shared she wanted Ralph to move on, free, so his soul would be released from the current bondage. I prayed with her for this release.

As I prayed I thought of how the Israelites, at the time, also in bondage, prayed for their freedom. I realized on some level we are all in chains, so to speak, and must ultimately free ourselves in order to evolve as both human beings as well as souls here as part of a greater order. During this time, I was preparing my home for Passover, which was just around the corner. All the teachings of freeing ourselves from bondage became reality as I watched Ralph's body and soul being imprisoned by the cancer, which was Ralph's "Pharaoh," or taskmaster, keeping him in captivity.

Though Shirley's tears were few, her eyes appeared very tired, and her face exposed the inner pain. Her acute grief had begun several months ago and, on a subtle level, I felt as if her readiness to release her beloved Ralph was encouraging him, though tiring. I asked her if she could think of any unfinished business Ralph might have left undone that could be postponing his desire to truly let himself go. She said he was very content, and cleared all of his business in preparation for this day.

She said, however, with a nervous laugh and eyeing me a bit more closely now, the only thing she could think of is that he'd remained sorry he never completed his *bar mitzvah*. This resonated deeply with me as extraordinarily important for Ralph. I requested of Shirley to have her sons present in the hospital room the next day, at 10 a.m.; Ralph was going to be a *bar mitzvah*! He would literally be called to the Torah and have one of his sons act as his representative. She smiled and agreed.

As I traveled the path to the hospital the next morning, joyfully hugging the *Sefer Torah* as I walked, the sun was shining brightly and the birds greeted me with a beautiful melody. Upon arriving at the hospital, inspired and feeling quite elated for engaging this ceremony for Ralph and, truly, his family, I entered the elevator to go to room 408. The *Etz Chaim*, the two wooden posts around which the Torah scroll is wrapped, were sticking out prominently, peeking through the *tallit* that covered the Torah.

A woman on the elevator innocently inquired, "Excuse me, do you play the bagpipes?" I smiled as I answered, "Today I do!"

Entering Ralph's room, I noticed bright decorations that the staff had taped to the walls. His room, once staid, had been transformed into an environment for celebration to commemorate Ralph's *bar mitzvah* ceremony. The room was overflowing, full to capacity with Shirley, their sons, family and hospital staff.

I explained the intention of this mini-service, and its order. I asked the entire makeshift congregation to direct their loving awareness and well wishes to Ralph. I unwrapped the Torah from the *tallit* and called Ralph to the Torah. His oldest son proceeded to receive the honor for his father.

I read the *Sh'ma* passage from the Torah, encouraging Ralph to bask in these words, listening for the call of the angels that are welcoming him to join them in their joyful procession. As it was nearing Passover, the time we are annually "freed" from *Mitzrayim* ("Egypt," symbolic of the narrow places where we remain confined and constricted). I offered a short sermon. I explained that during our lives we are all placed in these narrow spaces and, with strength and faith, we have the capacity to be released from this constriction. I gave Ralph permission to fully free himself from and exit, once and for all, his *Mitzrayim* without any fear, to free his holy soul.

I continued, "We again stand before You --- Ralph and his family. Master of the Universe, forgive him anything he may have done, intentionally or unintentionally, to offend You or hurt any person or any thing in Your Universe. Let his soul be in Your deepest peace."

"Guard and keep watch over his family. Allow them inner peace, knowing he will be safe. Let Ralph feel confident that he did good deeds here on Your Earth during his lifetime and that his loved ones will be continuing his loving legacy, inspired and in robust health."

"I ask the Archangels --- Michael, Gavriel, Uriel and Rafael --- to surround him now and escort him into the arms of those who left the world before him, welcomed by those very souls now that love him. Send signs to his family that he is safe and in Your arms. Amen!"

I then asked all to join me as we recited the *Sh'ma prayer* together. The tears we all cried were those of sustained joy and poignant sorrow of those now missing a beloved presence. We raised the Torah, dressed it and wrapped it in the *tallit*.

I went over to Ralph, kissed him on his forehead and whispered to him, "*Mazel tov*, my dearest friend. You are a *bar mitzvah*."

Ralph died 10 minutes later.

May his memory be a blessing, and may the bagpipes always play his song!

From this I learned that we all have unfinished business which must be completed in our lives. We strive to complete everything, however, there is always something undone, as long as we are living. Some of these things are more important than others. Ralph taught me not to hesitate to complete the tasks that are in our grasp when we are able to do so. I take to heart the line from Psalm 90:12, "Teach us to treasure each day, so we may open our hearts to Your Wisdom."

Follow The Yellow Brick Road

Someday I'll wish upon a star
and wake up where the clouds are far behind me.
- Over the Rainbow

WE ARE ALL HOARDERS OF SOME KIND. Some of us hoard our possessions, some our money, and some, life itself. When a loved one has been declared "brain dead" and we are told by physicians that they will have no quality of life, how do we let them go so their body and soul will be released with dignity and their suffering will come to an end. This decision tears at our hearts, and at times, if there is no advanced directive, tears families apart.

Some religions dictate that it is a sin to "pull the plug." So, as natural hoarders, the most prized possession we want to hoard, is life itself. We are taught in the teaching from the *"Tur"*, written by Rabbi Yaakov ben Raash (Rabbi Jacob ben Asher), if there is no *quality* of life, there is no *life*. Prior to our modern technology and our ability to keep people breathing, therefore trapping their soul, people left the world naturally. I invite you to join Grace, in the story below, as she travels down the "Yellow Brick Road" during her struggle with "pulling the plug."

I WAS MAKING ROUNDS AT A HOSPITAL. Exiting the elevator, I rounded the corner leading to the cardiac unit and was quite surprised to be met with celebratory fanfare amongst the staff. The usually sterile and quiet hall was alive with celebration: balloons and an enormous cake that read,

"Happy Birthday Murray." I inquired who "Murray" was, and was promptly informed he is the patient in room number 607. The hall was alive with administrators, the CEO of the hospital, and news reporters, a very rare scene, I can assure you! I chose to visit other patients on the floor until the hoopla ceased. Only then, an hour or so later, I entered room 607.

After knocking on the door and receiving permission to enter, I walked into the room. A very short woman named Grace greeted me; she must have only been about three-feet-and-inches in height. Her bright, flowing clothing accentuated the radiant eyes that touched my heart with love and compassion. Her presence was that of a shining star. The room was filled with all kinds of medical equipment, most of which was attached somehow to the patient. Although it was gloomy and cloudy outside, a single ray of sunlight pierced through the clouds, illuminating Murray's face. Murray, Grace and I were alone in the room, as the celebration was now over.

In the bed I saw a man who must have once stood about the same height as Grace. Peeking through his covers I saw that the oxygen mask, which covered a good portion of his round face and bubbly cheeks.

I knew from reading his chart that he was suffering from a chronic heart disorder. His full head of hair was neatly combed and, though covered by the mask, I could make out his welcoming smile, a smile of contentment. The basic joyful presence of these two people negated the bleakness of the hospital room and made it come alive as if from within.

I introduced myself as the chaplain, and their greeting remained warm and inviting. I was told that today was Murray's eightieth birthday. I congratulated him, also wishing him a happy birthday, though they clearly deduced I was confused about the lavish celebration. Many patients had birthday parties while in the hospital, though none such as Murray's earlier. I was invited to sit by Grace and, accepting her invitation, she shared their story.

Murray was the last surviving "munchkin" from the 1939 film, "The Wizard of Oz." He's quite recognizable, acting to the right of Dorothy, played by none other than Judy Garland, as they skip down the yellow brick road. Grace went on to tell me how Murray was an entertainer all his life. He appeared in numerous films as well as starring on stage in the Catskill Mountains. She took out a picture book and shared pictures of his career, most of them from the forever popular film, "The Wizard of Oz." The pictures were of Murray with Dorothy, The Tin Man, The Scarecrow, The Lion and, of course, The Wizard himself. As she spoke she became more and more animated, joyful and proud. Murray was unable to respond verbally due to the oxygen mask, but he displayed his approval with gesturing excitedly. I was entering the world of feeling with this vibrant couple as their spirit came alive through the magic of a very-healthy sense of the living theater.

My mind was busy and overjoyed with the stories revealed in their scrapbook. I thought of the characters and the effect they have had upon so many of our lives. I was able to see these characters from a movie I had seen countless times in a new and very personal way. I realized I never took the time to fully explore the mythology of the landscape of Oz, let alone the souls of these characters, so to speak. "Yes," I reflected to myself, "I see in each of these characters of Oz a resounding need, something that would support their existence and ultimate quest in life, but what else?"

Murray and Grace's identities appeared in some way inseparable from the world and implications of the quest of Oz. I saw the Tin Man, now lying before me, who was in need of a heart. This Tin Man displayed compassion, concern and love for his friends, implying the heart he had was, in fact, much more significant and capable of a love that beautified him from the inside.

I saw the Scarecrow, who was in need of a brain, employing logic with clarity and understanding while masterminding the trip that would ultimately see this gang of holy fools to their quest for the grail: the Wizard.

I saw The Lion, lacking in courage, or so he says, but was strong and fearless, standing erect to protect his friends as they journeyed. Both Murray and Grace, though fearful of where Murray may be standing in his current journey, were clearly displaying an ultimate courage that was both inspiring and heartbreaking.

I saw Dorothy, the child in all of us that yearns so much for truth, justice and holiness in the world, running in all directions to find it.

I saw the Witches, one good and one evil, as our conflicted inner selves as we wrestle with our emotions, thoughts and temptations.

And I saw the Wizard. The Supreme Being we strive to be close to, that, though he may disappoint us, will always provide us with the ingredients to advance and go on to the highest levels. My thoughts took me to the place where all people see God, though in different ways --- and some, not at all. The characters on the path to the Wizard were seeking his wisdom, unaware that the wisdom, was not with the Wizard, but with all the characters they met along their journey. How wonderful it would be if we, in our daily lives, would stop, not judge, and listen to the holy characters that we meet along our yellow brick road. In the Torah, we learn from parsha Lech L'cha that God said to Abraham, "Go forth to the land that I will show you....and you shall be a blessing." We all travel a mysterious road that takes us from our comfort zone, our familiar home, to the place that God will reveal to us in order to come closer to the reality of our own selves.

We visited for only about an hour, but it felt like we had bonded in a way beyond the limitations of the clock. Though appearing short, these were spiritual giants. Their entire lives had been focused around this movie. Because the movie was an American icon, they attained celebrity status, which catapulted them into a lifelong career in the entertainment industry. When I noticed Murray fading into sleep, I took this as my cue to leave. First, I was inspired to offer a blessing:

"Murray, may you feel God's energy traveling through you as holy breath, bringing you the healing and sustenance you need to go on with your life and work. May the joy that you have brought to so many lives be realized for generations, and may you be healed in body, mind and spirit."

"Grace, may you have the inner and outer strength and courage to sustain your energy for yourself as well as to continue to be a support to Murray."

"May you both, together, walk in God's light. Amen."

We hugged each other and I left the room.

I visited Murray and Grace many more times over the following months. I felt a deep connection and profound respect for this family. It wasn't that I found them endearing as short people, or because they were famous, though both initially contributed to a sense of uniqueness and awe about them. It was because they were contagiously joyful and engaged in the practice of life *as art*. I felt drawn to them and left rewarded having connected with them as thoughtful and learned souls. As it happened, Murray recovered and left the Hospital.

Some months passed and, one day, as I was making my rounds in the Intensive Care Unit, and I saw Grace. She immediately informed me that Murray's condition had worsened and he was now in the ICU unit intubated on life support. We spoke for a while and she related that Murray's breathing was strained and he was visibly declining. As she spoke her hands trembled and her voice waivered. During this conversation, I noticed she was clutching her scrapbook, including all the pictures and articles they'd shared with me those months ago. She again shared these photographic memories with me and, listening, I knew that this scrapbook was the self-defined and manifest metaphor of their lives. I was immediately was brought back to the sacred space I shared with them during their previous time in the hospital. Grace held the book tightly to her heart.

I realized that this scrapbook Grace was holding was, in effect, her living sacred scroll. It contained the memories she and Murray had amassed over their life shared together. Upon seeing each photograph this inspired the immediate recollection of their lessons learned and wisdom obtained. Each picture was a story and each story contained many life lessons.

Days went on and Murray was not recovering. His internal systems had now shut down leaving his body bloated and unresponsive. The physicians told Grace that Murray was not going to recover this time and suggested they remove the life support that was keeping his body functioning. She adamantly refused this open for her beloved. She clung to her scrapbook and remained at Murray's side.

Eventually an ethics council was convened to explain the uselessness of continuation of life support. In spite of the concerted efforts of the hospital staff, Grace continued to refuse to consent. I was called and asked if I would communicate to Grace that the situation was hopeless. The staff knew of our relationship, and it was their hope she would listen to me.

I sat with Grace feeling torn between my duty as a staff member of the hospital and my commitment to Grace and Murray as friends. The meeting began intimately as we shared tears, a hug and concern for Murray. Again, now desperately, she opened her bound metaphor, full of images from their lives, and once again proceeded to tell me their story. She clutched the book tightly and I knew this was her way of holding on to Murray.

I sat and listened to Grace for nearly an hour without saying a word. Her tears were like a holy well of love traveling down her cheeks. She knew that there was no hope for Murray's recovery; however, her intense grief masked the reality that she needed to let him go. She knew Murray had no quality of life, and in essence his life had ended. When she had finished sharing those things she needed to say, I held her hand and explained the staff's diagnosis. We spoke of life, contrasted with quality-of-life, the possibility of Murray being trapped in his body and how special it would be to release his precious soul. She said she knew this had to be done, though she could not, and would not, give the order to kill him. I looked into her eyes and felt a strong attachment to her soul.

"Grace," I said, "Murray's soul is in black and white. Let it go to Technicolor." Our eyes met with intensity, and at that moment, I knew that she knew with absolute truth and clarity that she needed to let go of Murray. I felt blessed that the words came to me which shifted her thinking. I knew that I had to make a connection for Grace that would resonate with her present reality and their lives together. With tears flowing down her small puffy, red cheeks, she squeezed my hand, and asked if I would be present and recite a prayer when they discontinued life support. I agreed. "May he rest in peace, may his memory be a blessing, and may he always travel the 'Yellow Brick Road.' "

*   *   *

There is a deep lesson in this story that most of us will have to learn and face. The lesson is about the decisions we must make at the end of our lives, including those of our loved ones. When we enter a hospital we are asked, "what kind of insurance do you have," and, "do you have an advanced directive." The latter is such an important document as it legally declares your intention as to whether to wish to be treated or not at the end of life. If we are to find ourselves in the state that Murray was, and there was no directive, our families must make this decision for us. I have been with many families and for years, after making this decision, they will say, "I killed my loved one." As an advocate for advanced directives, I ask all to employ one, not for the sake of the hospital and the related staff, but for the sake of those we love most.

Section III.

Helping The Other On Their Own Terms
& Not Judging

I BELIEVE WE ARE ALL GUILTY OF JUDGING in various forms. We like to believe we have no prejudices however, being human, we do. In chaplaincy I hear many tales pertaining to the details of family dynamics. It is sometimes difficult not to judge and I make every attempt to place my judgments aside while engaging my duty. The stories in this section are lessons about not judging the other, but more intimately, joining with them, compassionately seeking to understand. By embracing the various preferences, points-of-view and even culture of others, one is able to grow and act on a level more closely bound up with the "holy" than simply the mundane.

The Gypsy Princess

AS A CHAPLAIN, I am introduced to people of many cultures --- some of whom are far away from my comfort zone and my day-to-day reality. My training has afforded me the honor of stepping into and sharing the cultural connection of patients who are part of exotic, exceptional and holy communities. I have learned that people of different cultures act and react to illness and death in different ways --- ways that metabolize with the history and customs of their community. At times, I have been invited by Muslim brothers to join them on their prayer rug. I have baptized infants, when on call in the middle of the night, by meditating and asking the spirit of Jesus to come through me so I could be the representative for the grieving parents. I have wrestled with many Hispanic families who grieve with loud shrieks and roll on the floor. When I began to learn, Reb Zalman told me whenever I go to a new city, I should stop in at the local ashram and seek out the Jewish residents who are searching for spirituality. I realized that his directive was not only for the ashrams, but also for all cultures in general. In order to join, we must understand. I have realized that all people who are true believers have the essence of God in their souls. I am privileged to join with them.

THERE WAS AN INCREDIBLE DISTURBANCE   outside one of the hospital units. I was called to assist. Upon arriving I was told that a gypsy princess --- yes, a gypsy princess, whose father happened to be King of the Gypsies for that region --- was recently admitted into the hospital. There were gypsies pouring into the hospital from all directions. These gypsies set themselves up and were actually camping on the hospital grounds, imbuing the surrounding area with a feeling as though a pilgrimage were taking place.

The hospital administration expressed concern that this crowd had begun stealing articles from the gift shop and, at the very least, were accused of creating a constant disturbance by their overwhelming presence. Ultimately, I was not asked to offer spiritual care for the patient but to report any acts of theft to security personnel, if needed.

As there were no "acts of theft" occurring as best as I could tell, I had plenty of time to observe what was unfolding at the hospital. For an institution that follows a fairly predictable schedule, though the details may prove more dramatic and intense at times, this was proving to be quite an extraordinary exception to the rule. At a certain point I wondered, "are we programmed to fear people and cultures with which we are not familiar?" I then thought of *Parshat Shelach*: Spies are being sent out by Moses, at the instruction of God, to explore the land that the Hebrew people are to travel through. The spies are terrified at the ways of this unfamiliar culture, ultimately returning with a false report. The spies share, upon returning, *there are giants in the land that will devour us*, and warning, *we must not enter*. The spies continue to warn that *the land will swallow up our lives and spirit if we enter*. I believe this biblical report resembles (and, as such, has an encoded message of warning to us) the report I received from the hospital administration. Thankfully I intuited I must investigate such claims and concerns for myself.

I was looking for facts --- there had to be more to this story, and I believed that my assignment was not to merely follow these people to assure administration they were not pilfering. I believed our paths came together from a divine space. I went to the patient's room. I was informed that the patient, a twenty-two year old woman, had cystic fibrosis. She was intubated. The disease had destroyed her lungs and she would not survive the removal of the tube. Familiarizing myself with the facts, I was able to approach the family.

I entered a waiting area where there were no less than thirty people congregating. I introduced myself. I was greeted with some nods, however nobody spoke with me. I passed through the crowd and entered the room of the young woman. Her name was Hilda. The room was filled with life saving equipment. The intravenous pole was supporting many bottles of medication, with hoses that led to the arm of the patient. The woman was lying motionless in bed. Her long black curls surrounded her face, and her engaging brown eyes peeked through the bright colored blankets. There were colored fringes coming from beneath the blanket. Over her, hanging like a mobile, there was a string that contained a beer bottle, a pair of shoes, a pack of cigarettes, and some other ornaments that I later found to be traditional Gypsy healing tools.

Men surrounded her bed. There were no women present. I introduced myself as the Chaplain. An older gentleman greeted me warmly. He wore a flannel shirt that was tucked neatly into his khaki pants, which were supported by wide dark blue suspenders. He wore brightly shined boots that came to a huge point at the toe. His vest was made of the finest silk and was completely hand embroidered. I wanted one exactly like it. His aura was that of a distinguished gentleman. He identified himself as the woman's father. I knew from prior knowledge that he was the Gypsy king. I told him it was an honor to meet him and offered my compassion for his daughter and his family. I gave him the honor I would extend to any person of high office I would meet. We spoke at length of his daughter's condition and prognosis. I asked if I could offer a blessing for her. My request was granted.

"Master of our Universe, I stand with the family of Hilda, one of your precious children who will soon join you. Please give her the strength and energy to open her heart to her that she may know how special and meaningful her life, although short, is to all of the family. Allow her to feel the love they send her allow her not to be in fear. Let her always walk arm in arm with your angels. Make the space for this holy family and tribe to celebrate life and be free of the labels that have shadowed their life style. Amen."

After I offered prayer, I asked if we could speak outside. Her father told me that he was not able to leave the bedside. He said that it is the belief of the Gypsy when a person is facing death, they must be surrounded at all times by those closest to them. He told me that it is their belief that precisely the moment of death the last person they breathe on will gain all of their knowledge. This is their way of passing wisdom.

I thought of Torah, *l'dor v'dor*, "from generation to generation." The importance of humanity standing on the shoulders of our ancestors transcends time and space – the teaching that we are an important link with the past and into the future. We must learn from the old, live in the present, in order to create the new.

I realized that this family was observing religious practice. I wanted to honor them with honesty so I told the son about the theft concern. I was assured me that there was no theft going on. He said the many people were present out of respect and they would not prostitute this respect with theft. At that moment I knew that there was no theft happening or about to happen. His eyes told me this was so. The theft threat was the administration's inability to take the time and learn this people's cultural differences.

I thought of how many lives over the centuries have been lost because of this same reason. They were being denied freedom of movement without suspicion. I spoke with the administrators and assured them there was no theft. They told me I would be responsible if there was. I looked directly into their eyes and walked away. It was ironic that the administrators were in greater fear of losing something material, than these holy people were of death.

Time passed and I saw the family at least twice per day. They grew to know me, and trust me. I sat in the waiting room and spoke with the people who initially snubbed me. I learned some of their prayer ritual, and prayed with them. Their way of prayer was not really different than mine. They created the same holy space as we all have, however they took a differed route. The only person I was not able to connect with was the woman's mother. Each time I approached her she would look down and spit on my shoes. After a while, I finally accepted this strange act without asking why it was so.

The days passed and the woman's father summoned me. He said it was time to remove life support, and he would like me present. I walked with him near the room. Her brother was there and a man I had not noticed. He came out and introduced himself. He was a short man, in simple dress, however his eyes were intense and told the Universe that he was holy. "My name is Ya'akov. I am the Priest." Although we had not met, he was aware of each motion and prayer I had said in the previous weeks. In a commanding voice he said, "You will be by my side as they disconnect the life support. You will pray with me." I thanked him, the father and brother for including me, "However," I said, "I would rather wait just outside the room." I was not a member of their tribe. Ya'akov glared at me with his huge dark eyes. He said nothing for a few moments and I was feeling tense. He then took my arm and said while gently tugging me toward the room, "We walked into the gas chamber together as brothers, we will be together now."

We prayed together and I was privileged to join in the traditional *vidui*, the end of life prayer, used specifically by this tribe of gypsies. I had entered holy space.

After the young Gypsy woman died her mother approached me. She explained that her way of mourning was not to engage in any talk. She said she had to be in complete silence in order to clear a connection and create a path to her ancestors for her daughter. She said the community knew not to approach her, however, to those outside the community; she would spit on their shoe. She thanked me for my prayers and concern for her family. The father said "Shalom Rabbi; live in peace." I wished him the same.

This family had taught me much about respect, acceptance, dedication and love. They authenticated their faith through living action. They opened the path for me to become closer to my own heart, breaking down the barriers the outside world had taken so long to erect within me, and we became partners. I was saddened to see them leave as I felt so close to them, however I thanked the Holy One of Blessing for the opportunity. I also said a prayer for the administrators to not be in fear of cultures other than their own.

Holy Smoke

WHEN A PERSON BECOMES ILL their beliefs dictate various customs for healing. Some of these customs are from ancient philosophies and some are from modern ways of life. I believe that when these beliefs and practices emerge from the heart they are all valid. The following tale is about a Native American patient who requested me to engage the healing prayers taught to him by his ancestors. Some healing methods may seem strange when they are unfamiliar, however their intention connects with the deepest place of healing in the patient's soul.

AS A RABBI, I READ AND STUDY Torah, Kabbalah, Psalms, Talmud and the Midrash (the collected interpretations of the rabbis on the dictates of *halachah*, or, law) of both our traditional and Hasidic sages, as well as more contemporary teachers and progressive thinkers. To share with you personally, this time spent in study and prayer --- the two going hand in hand, as a type of Jewish-centric *Lectio Divina* --- opens a corridor for me to reach the Sacred, my inner-core of spirituality, which *in*-spires my soul. It is this field of the sacred which I seek to cultivate and, therefore, able to harvest the fruits of my labor to share with others, to stay with the metaphor. My focused time spent in study and prayer in this way offers a sense of freedom and renewal I invest in that further allows me to maintain my balance as a "normal" person with that of acting as a chaplain and answering my vocational call. From this time spent being renewed and inspired I can most directly access the words of the *Sh'ma, Echad*, "We *are* One," and return to engaging the world knowing, having felt the truth, we *are* all One *with* God. Our source and destination is the same though we all travel unique paths in between.

I was called into the room of Ron, a Native American man from the Lakota tribe. He had been very ill and tests were being conducted to determine the cause of his illness. While I visited with him he spoke very directly, as if his heart were speaking. "I know you are a rabbi and I am familiar with the *mi'shebarach, your* healing prayer. I am also familiar with the sacrament of the sick offered by Christians, and the healing chants by Buddhists. I would like you to assist me in my healing prayer. It is called smudging."

I inquired further how the smudging ceremony is traditionally offered to one in need. He taught me, "You will take a shell and place tobacco, sage and other herbs into it. You grind them together and light the combination of herbs until it begins to smolder. When the smoke grows thick you direct it around the room with this feather." He pulled a beautiful undecorated black feather with white tips from the wrapping of a fine cloth. "As you direct the smoke with the feather, I will chant the ancient melody of my people for healing." He had all the ingredients brought to him by a friend earlier that day.

Taking the necessary precautions for, essentially, lighting a fire in a room not previously designated for such ceremonies, I called the hospital security and asked them to temporarily shut down the smoke alarm and sprinkler system in his room. The head-nurse placed a "Do Not Disturb" sign on the door for our privacy.

While I was preparing the space, Ron was mixing the tobacco and herbs in the shell. I turned the lights off and I lit the shell as instructed. A sweet yet earthy aroma soon enveloped the room. As the smoke began to rise, I carefully, and with the intention for healing, directed the shamanic clouds over his body with the feather. Ron began to chant. Though I did not understand the words, I knew they were holy and had a mission shared with those words I utter when engaging my personal devotions. As the smoke and its fragrance filled the room, the beautiful song of Ron's chanting emanated as if from his soul. His chant was piercing and holy. The ceremony we engaged in together lasted only about twenty minutes.

This was a profoundly sacred experience for me. I felt healed, but also connected to a higher power, what I've connected to through *Echad*, in a way I had not experienced before. My eyes watered, teary not from the smoke but from its intention. I hugged Ron, thanking him for inviting me into his sacred space and sharing this beautiful ceremony with me. He looked me in the eyes and said, "You are my brother." I felt that this connection with Ron was a great honor bestowed upon me. My thoughts returned back to my many meetings with Reb Shlomo Carlebach as he would look into everyone's eyes, and say "Holy Brother (or Holy Sister), you are the holiest person in the world". At first, I thought this seemed insincere, but later came to believe that in that moment, we were indeed, "the holiest". As I met many friends over the years, I now refer to them as my holy brother or sister. So, when Ron addressed me as his brother, I was able to join my soul with his, as family.

I left the room and, after advising security that we were finished and they could reinstate the security in the room, I sat down looked to the clear sky. *"Echad,"* I quietly said. Indeed, we are One. Ron had a full recovery and we remained friends. I have attended sweat lodges with him and was asked to pray with his friends as we sweated together. I have brought and blown the *shofar* for my new friends on several occasions now so they may hear its sounds, and they have shared their sacred instruments with me, such as the flute and drum.

I believe we should not invest in the fear of the unknown because, truly, all is unknown waiting to be revealed to us. When we open ourselves to the outside world and, therefore, that which initially strikes us as "unknown," what may at one point seem strange becomes intimately familiar soon after, and may even become sacred. Our soul has traveled many paths over many incarnations. In order for our most profound soul to expand we must create the space for it to explore. I believe when we reach a deep space of meditation, or just before falling asleep, or during deep sleep, our souls travel. We typically cannot remember our soul visions while traveling. Sometimes we are hit with the sensation of *déjà vu*, which I believe is a spark from our travels through time and space, which has entered into our reality. Sometimes we meet a person who looks intimately familiar, yet we've not met before --- a meeting from another time and space? Our deepest friendships, oftentimes deeper than family connections are with our soul friends, those we feel the most comfortable with - those with whom we can share the truths of our hearts. My blessing is for all of us to be able to find and recognize members of our soul family in our lifetime.

Hallelujah

EVEN THOUGH I HAVE BEEN CALLED UPON many times in my career to enter an unfamiliar home, with customs that are radically different from my own, I am always delighted and amazed when I can join with community and family and help to create sacred space. When a beloved African American matriarch died, I was privileged to witness the honor bestowed upon her memory by her family, friends and community via storytelling, singing and prayer.

I WAS IN A DEEP SLEEP when I heard the pager go off. I glanced at the clock on my night table. It read 3 a.m. I stumbled to the telephone and, reaching the hospital, was told me there had been a death and a family was in need of immediate spiritual support. They gave me the address. I had just enough time to wash my face, throw on some clothes and rush out the door. As I drove I gradually woke up realizing the address was in one of the more violent neighborhoods where there were often shootings and robberies. I was afraid to proceed, though I knew I had to go, answering a greater need than my early-morning fear.

Once I had arrived I locked my car doors as I searched for house numbers, standing in the dark and desolate streets of this Miami neighborhood. The houses were dilapidated, as if crumbling before my very eyes. There were no streetlights --- at least none lit --- and it felt as if I had entered a third world country. Signs of apparent poverty and neglect were everywhere.

As I oriented myself, my thoughts turned to the people in our world that are oppressed, rarely enjoying the surplus so many of us take for granted. How can we, a nation of plenty, allow this to happen on such a broad scale at home, let alone abroad, globally? I was aware of this as a general phenomenon, but now I found myself shaken, present in a neighborhood where the richest country in the world had clearly failed its people sworn to protect.

As I approached the house there was a group of people in the street, probably thirty or so who had gathered to pay their respects I made my way through the crowd to the doorstep. The door was open, there being quite a bit of activity even though it was still quite early in the morning, and I entered the house, introducing myself as the chaplain. The house was decorated neatly, the furniture reminding me of my grandmother's house when I was growing up in Philadelphia. I was warmly greeted and escorted to the room where the body was lying.

In the bed I saw an elderly woman who had lived past ninety years. Her frail body was almost transparent, revealing her bones. Strands of gray knotty hair covered her eyes, and she had the obvious and beautiful appearance of contentment on her face. I went to her side and invited the immediate family present in the house to join me.

The family spoke of her with love and respect, sharing with me how she had been the matriarch of the family. The family recounted she was the one who had taught them about love, respect, dignity and honor and the import of such elegance of character in one's life. She taught them right from wrong, always speaking of how lucky they were to have all that they had, and the blessings their life graced them with to live with such freedom. She never complained when she came home from work after cleaning other people's houses all day. She had clearly provided for all her family's physical and emotional needs. They loved her dearly and this was obviously a devastating loss now that Millie had passed.

As an interfaith Chaplain, I am often called upon to say prayers for other faiths. We all gathered at bedside and joined hands as I led this family in a bed-side prayer. I closed my eyes, took a moment to reflect, and asked the Holy One to focus my attention so that I could sincerely be the representative for Jesus and that my prayer should be authentic to his word.

"Jesus, before us is Your Millie. Her soul has come to join with You and Your Father. Please, open your arms and welcome her into Your garden. Let her be greeted by the familiar faces of her ancestors and friends. Allow her soul the rest knowing she did well for her family, living integrally with her values as an example for the following generations. Let her family be able to teach the quest of freedom that she had to endure to their children, grandchildren and great-grandchildren. Send your angels to escort her through the 'valley of the shadow of death' without fear. Allow her family to know she is safe, in Your arms, and bless her soul with peace." At this point I asked the family to join me in reciting The Lord's Prayer.

After completing my paperwork and waiting for the funeral home to pick Millie up, I sat with this wonderful family, listening to them sharing about their stories of their life with Millie. Everyone in the home had a relevant and beautiful story about Millie. She was clearly a righteous woman. I hugged and offered a final blessing.

I started to walk to my car noticing now there were well over sixty people in the street. I was no longer in fear of this foreign environment and these individuals I didn't know --- it had melted away in the presence of this generous family. Millie's oldest son took my arm as I made my way down the sidewalk and asked that I please join them, those that had gathered in this group. We formed a large circle, holding hands in the street. We sang songs of praise --- old-fashioned gospel songs to Jesus and to God --- the celebratory tone of these emotional songs carried our voices high, as if we were escorting Millie to sacred lands. My soul was completely opened as I became part of the extended family of these people. I feared them a few hours ago and now we traveled together into a holy spiritual space. Time stopped. When I did return to my car it was about 6 a.m. Surprisingly, I was not the least bit tired but felt a sense of aliveness, renewed by the experience of the morning. I felt that I did not have to recite my traditional prayers this morning as prayers of another kind had taken the place of my routine. I had already prayed to God with new friends but with a shared voice.

Making my way back home I reflected on the nature of fear and the effect it can have on us. I was taught when we are in fear, it drowns our heart and we do not function appropriately. I was taught this is a death, of sorts, on all levels, *especially* on the spiritual level. I also reflected further on the nature of judgment and the unjust act of judging people. I *had* judged these people only because they appeared "poor" and did not readily display the "luxuries" to which I was accustomed. How arrogant of me! As it would turn out, this morning I was introduced to wealth and celebratory luxury that, all these years later as I recount this tale, am still deriving inspiration from! We sometimes say it, but we rarely actualize living the truth: we are all holy. Beneath the superficialities lies the inner core and the spark of holiness we all embody. It is this inner core that is our shared truth. My *Hallel* prayer (a prayer derived from the Psalms), although having different words, is functionally the same as theirs, shared above.

In the deepest part of our souls, the place where the superficial trappings of neighborhood, skin color, religious or ethnic identities can be bypassed, is the only place where we can all connect in "oneness."

The Clubhouse Turn

SOMETIMES I MEET PEOPLE who have lived their lives, "on the edge." They have breached relationships with family, have habits that are barely legal, have personalities that are harsh, they may even seem unlovable at first and are looked upon negatively by common societal standards. They, too, get sick and come to the end of their life. Are they not entitled to leave the world in dignity with the pleasures they enjoyed while in the prime of their life too?

I WAS MAKING MY ROUNDS, visiting a nursing home, and was asked by a staff member to speak with Max, one of the residents. I entered the room and found him in a chair reading the sports page of a local paper. A frail man, his six-foot frame must have only totaled about one-hundred pounds. His drawn cheeks revealed a bony face and toothless mouth. His legs were wire-thin, even skeletal, unable to support his own body.

He introduced himself to me by saying, "Leon, right? You have to lose some weight. You're too damn fat!"

"You're right. I wish I could give some to *you*!"

We both laughed and I sat down, asking him how he was doing today.

"How should I be doing? I'm stuck here in this cage." He went on to tell me about his life.

"You know, I was a street guy. I gambled, whored around, took drugs --- I was one of the 'wise guys.' I was respected on the street, you know? My friends were loan sharks, bookies, con artists and number writers. Those were the days..." He recounted many stories, many of them quite gruff. As he spoke further of the "good ol' days," he gained energy and became much more animated. We visited for a long time and the stories flowed out of Max as if I was watching a noir film being recounted.

"So, tell me Max, you are a hospice patient and you are aware you are approaching the end of your life. Is there anything I can offer you at this time?" I can't heal you, but for some reason I like crusty old men. So, tell me, what do you need brother --- I'm here". He looked into my eyes and chuckled.

"I used to hang out at the track every day. I met my friends there and I knew all the horses and jockeys. That was my home. I have no family --- the people at the track were my family. I'll tell you what I need: one more day at the track, a pack of cigarettes and some gambling money!" I found myself unable to directly respond to this surprising request of Max's. I told him I would stop and see him again next week. I did not directly respond to his request, however, I was thinking, "why not"?

"This was a good meeting, thanks, Leon. I like you." He said.

I left his room, his stories dominating my thoughts over the course of the day. What could I do for this unique character? I called the local racetrack and told them Max's story. The public relations woman was touched. She said, "Why don't you bring him here as our guest? We will make sure he has a seat in the clubhouse and treat him to lunch." I told her I would try and arrange it. I then contacted the nursing home to see if this was feasible. They were excited and said they would provide transportation and an aid. I confirmed a date and went to tell Max it was all set. He could not believe it. I thought he was going to leap from the bed and bear hug me. The excitement filled his entire being.

"Hey Leon, don't forget the cigs!" I laughed as I left Max's room.

The big day was upon us. I picked Jackie up at home --- she had never been to a racetrack --- as I wanted to share this day with her. On the way to the nursing home, we stopped at a convenience store to purchase a pack of Marlboro "100's," his preferred cigarettes.

The CEO of the nursing home decided to join us and bring four other patients who she knew would appreciate the day. It was a very unusual scene as the patients filed into the van, toting their oxygen tanks, occupying wheel chairs and yielding canes, all of us bound for the horse track. As we arrived at the track, we were directed to the designated VIP parking lot, met by a representative from the Public Relations department. She introduced herself and told us she would be our escort throughout the day. Upon entering the track she escorted us to the clubhouse where we were to sit for the day. Max surprised us all by saying this would not work for him. He informed us that his seats were down by the midway where he could remain close to the action.

"That's my hangout," pointing to seats closer to the track. We proceeded there.

As we settled into our seats our escort handed Max a program and said to him, "Mr. Schwartz, you might want to look at the fifth race in particular." He opened the program and, in bold print it read, "The Max Schwartz Handicap." His eyes became bright in disbelief. She also told him he would be escorted to the winner's circle after the fourth race to present the trophy to the jockey. His smile, like a Cheshire Cat's, was larger than his face! It was a beautiful scene as the day unfolded.

We had all chipped in some money so Max would be able to place a bet on the races. He was too weak to walk to the window, so he picked the horses and we placed his bets for him. He inspected the bet stubs to make sure his bets had been placed correctly, the ashes from his cigarettes dropping on to his lap. After losing the first three races he smiled and said, "It's like old times. I lose every race," and, clearly happy with the result, added, "all is in perfect harmony!" The pari-mutuel board lit up for the fourth race. The top of the board read in enormous letters, "The Max Schwartz Handicap."

Max stared at the board with contagious joy, a toothless smile encompassing his entire face. No words were necessary. The bugler stepped out to blow the horn for the race. He was dressed in the colorful attire of the track: a red formal jacket and black pants were tucked into his high boots. The announcer proclaimed, "Ladies and gentlemen, welcome to the Max Schwartz Handicap of four furlongs!" Max leaned back in his wheelchair, his Marlboro cigarette hanging off the side of his mouth. The contentment apparent on his face illuminated what he was feeling.

"And they're off!" Max hung on to every call from the announcer.

When the race was complete he was, in fact, escorted to the winner's circle. He presented the trophy to the jockey and had his picture taken with the horse, the owner and the jockey.

We stayed for one more race. Max began to lose his energy and, after a long but hugely rewarding day, it was time to leave.

The following week I went to the nursing home to bring pictures my wife had taken. Max's bed was empty. His body was absent and I immediately saw his soul remaining back at the horse track.

Though I personally did not agree with the life style Max had chosen, it was also not my duty to judge him. I was present to help him with closure so he could leave our world in peace. A copy of the picture from the track was placed in his coffin.

I sincerely believe that when we honor another's needs, we are also recognizing our own needs. We have a tendency to judge people. If we are able to release that need within ourselves we will be granted the ability to see more clearly. Max reaffirmed the truth within me that says, "Be who you are, and not who you are expected to be."

In my ministry I meet people from a multi-faceted socio economic background; from those who are millionaires, to middle class working people, to those like Max, who are down and out. I strive to reach each person, at their own level, so I might help them either recover from their illness, or help them with their transition, giving them some joy and laughter along the way. Max died without money, but he accumulated a wide circle of friends who appreciated him, for who he was. He died being his own true self. The story of Reb Zushia is a tender lesson that I believe Max would have appreciated:

When I die and come before the heavenly court, if they ask me, "Zushia, why were you not like Abraham?" I'll say, "I didn't have Abraham's intellectual abilities." If they say, "Why were you not like Moses?" I'll say, "I didn't have Moses' leadership abilities." For every such question, I'll have an answer. But if they say, "Why were you not Zushia?" For that, I'll have no answer.

Here Comes The Sun

If I am not for myself, who will be for me?
And, if I am only for myself, what am I?
If not now, when?

- Pirke Avot, 1:14

THE WORD, *"TESHUVA,"* IN HEBREW is often translated as the noun, "repentance." However, the translation that we are taught in rabbinics is the verb, "to return." A person once asked Reb Pinchas of Koretz, an early nineteenth century Hasidic rabbi, about the nature of good and evil and how we, as people, are able to help balance the scales, so to speak. He taught, "Imagine the entire world is equal in good and evil and you are on a tightrope attempting to balance them. You are the deciding factor for the entire Universe. All creation is resting on you. Which way do you proceed?"

I am a frequent viewer of "Law & Order: Special Victims Unit." The prelude to each episode concludes with the words "heinous act" which is followed by a loud, ominous sounding musical note, preparing us for the show we are about to see. The musical note only lasts for a second, however, the darkness and dread that the viewer knew they would be encountering wasn't real --- after all, this was only a television show. For me, however, this expectation of dread became part of my psyche, and followed me throughout in the story that follows.

THE EARLY MORNING SUN had just emerged, and I was preparing for a day of peace and harmony. Even though I knew that my written daily schedule often varies from the reality of my patient's unexpected requests, I was hopeful that I could adhere to a simple schedule without major calamities. Eager to begin my rounds, I delayed so I could meditate and reflect as the brightness of the sun danced across my face filling my soul-batteries as if I, too, was a type of solar panel --- a solar panel of the Divine! I was caught off guard as the pager went off: *Beep, beep, beep!* My heart skipped a beat as the pager interrupted the calmness I was enjoying vanished.

I was summoned to a man who was fast approaching his death and wished to have the end of life prayers recited at his bedside. The man was of Christian faith, so I meditated for the energy of his faith to travel through me in order to properly represent him with the Holy One of Blessing. I found a private unoccupied small room nearby and asked the Holy One for the words and guidance to come to me so I could honor his spiritual space and beliefs with integrity.

I approached the room yet was stopped by a police officer that was stationed outside. He inquired who I was and what business I had with the dying man. Naturally I identified myself and shared with the officer the dying man's requested bedside prayer. The officer said, "Don't go in there! The scum doesn't deserve our prayers. Let him die and go straight to hell." I was taken back and asked why he was so angry. He said that Stan, the man in the bed, was a child molester. Stan was convicted of molesting and torturing several children between the ages of seven and eleven. "Let him die without prayers."

I was stunned and my mind began to run away with thoughts. I am the father of three and a grandfather.. I imagined how I would feel if it were one of my own children who had suffered the horrendous abuse of this man. Over the years my wife and I have saved numerous at-risk kids, helping to redirect them in the right direction for a potentially more meaningful life. To say I was livid would be an understatement. I was angry with this man and what he had done, and at the same time I was angry with myself for judging and allowing my emotion to block the mission with which I was entrusted. I was burning with fury and confusion as I turned away and left the floor. The note of dread engulfed me and I felt stunned, as if being hit by a lightning rod. My anger was intense, and although knowing had to manage it, I was unsure as to how to get it under control.

I continued on my usual rounds, as I attempted to fool myself into believing all was fine and as it should be in the universe when, in fact, at least concerning my orbit, it was not. As I entered each room on my rounds the sunshine through the window seemed to follow me. It made no difference which way I was facing. I could not escape the sun. It was reminding me of the tranquility I was feeling earlier that morning. It was reminding me I had a mission. It was a potent aide of the teaching of Reb Pinchas of Koretz. I was now in charge of the balance of the world. I was unable to control the tears as they began to flow. I went into a quiet room, and lost all power over my tears. There was no escape. I was imprisoned by my emotions. Fear, anger and judgment had taken over my being, as I knew I had to return to Stan's guarded hospital room.

Approaching the room once again, the officer confronted me again. He said, "What are you doing back? I told you about this creep!" I ignored him and entered the room, having clearance to do so. Although frail, Stan's disease had reduced his weight to about ninety pounds, and unable to move, he was, nevertheless, handcuffed to the rails on the bed. He had tubes and intravenous tubes extending out from his arm. He was clearly in a great deal of pain.

The room was dark and a tree veiled the sun that haunted me the entire day. His words were strained as his voice was reduced to a whisper. I leaned over the bed. He whispered in my ear. "I know what I did and I am sorry.

God is punishing me now and I deserve what I am getting. How do I tell God I am sorry and pray for the children I violated before I die?"

I thought of my many lessons of *teshuva or repentance*. I responded to his request, "Stan, you have asked for forgiveness. But, will you be forgiven?" I told him I could not say that, because I do not know. "Your soul will discover this when it is released from your body." He looked me in the eye, and asked if I would pray with him. I took a deep breath, a hard swallow, and began to pray:

"God, I am here with Stan. He has dishonored his existence on Earth with many terrible transgressions. He now requests forgiveness and guidance from you. He also seeks Your protection as well as Your healing for the children that he violated. You are all-merciful, God. Hear his plea and take him to Your womb. Restore and heal his soul when it arrives in your care." Stan and I said, "amen," and he thanked me for coming.

When I went into his room, I entered with hate in my heart because of his terrible deeds, but I knew I had to pray for his soul. My thoughts shifted from the prayer I offered Stan to me. Intellectually, I knew I needed to transcend my anger, but emotionally, I was stuck. I was more concerned about my own integrity by having to offer an end of life prayer, than of Stan's tortured soul. Being ordained as a "Master of the Blessing", I am responsible to offer blessings that people need. Was I being a phony?

Outside the guard took my arm, "Are you happy that you gave that creep absolution? You should be ashamed of yourself." I sat next to him and placed my hand with his. "I did not give him absolution. Only God could grant that. I merely served as a go-between, a representative that allowed him to express his feelings." I looked into the guard's eyes. They were burning with anger. "I bless you to be able to perform your duties with the same conviction I was able to perform mine. I bless you not to judge, but to direct your energy for the side of the good. I bless you to feel whole inside your soul. I bless you with peace."

I asked the guard to say, "amen." He refused and I slowly made my way down the hall.

I again sat with sun shining on my face. I was sitting in the beautiful meditation garden near the hospital's entranceway. More tears came, however they were different from tears earlier. These were tears of an inner peace and relief. I thought of how we judge others and how we judge ourselves. We are creatures of habit and we will continue to judge regardless of how we attempt not to do so. Do we have to forgive in order to create the balance that Reb Pinchas speaks about in his teaching? I do not know the answer. However, I do believe we must maintain our own balance, for the sake of the greater balance of our collective souls in this world. For now, our task is to figure out what true balance is and the proper way to travel the tightrope.

As we know, the sun is our greatest energy source. It followed me the entire day and evaded all my attempts to not let it shine in my eyes. Unbeknownst to me, this glare that I was attempting to avoid, was recharging my spiritual batteries.

During the writing of this story, I have a sense that hundreds of innocent children, if not thousands, were being abused verbally or physically. Our society's scandals with child molestation are horrific, and are out of control. We know that abuse is covered up, swept under the rug for the sake of not shaming the community embroiled in the scandals. Oftentimes justice does not prevail, letting criminals continue with their lives and ruining the lives of children, forever. I have hundreds of stories to tell that could have been included in this book. I chose to include this sorrowful tale to bring awareness, and hopefully action, by the proper authorities regarding this ongoing horror. No more cover-ups. When a child or a parent reports abuse, they must be heard.

My actions and reactions to this situation weighed heavily on me for several days. My duties as a Chaplain dictated that I recite a prayer for this person, however, I was feeling unsettled. The edges of my soul felt frayed and dismayed. And then, as if so often happens, a friend shared a relevant teaching with me, this time from Rabbi Arthur Green's book, "Ehyeh" from the chapter, "What About Evil."

The soul within us remains pure; even the greatest sinner, the doer of the most heinous deeds, has a pure soul. To gain access to that unsullied self requires great, sometimes super-human effort. Teshuvah, *the process of return and transformation, is not to be taken lightly.*

This man was attempting to do *teshuvah* in order for him to return to the Holy One with peace; I was merely his vehicle.

Section IV.

Doing The Right Thing By Breaking Rules

ONE OF MY FAVORITE VERSES from the Torah is, "You have a choice to be a blessing or a curse, be a blessing --- choose life" (Deuteronomy 11:26). The stories you will read in this section are about choices, some positive and some negative. As you read the stories in this section, my hope is for you to think about the choices you have made, and will make, in your life. Think about what drives us to the choices we make and how it interacts with who we are and who we will become.

In order to become a Board Certified chaplain, I took two years of intense training in both clinical intensives as well as the standard classroom-based education. My weekly "verbatims," the times I was training as a chaplain working with clients, were recorded and later dissected by my peers, supervisors and me. Upon finishing my intensive clinical, I was preparing to go before the panel of people I had never met.

Some of my peers, who were also friends, convened a mock panel to better prepare me. After about two hours of back and forth questions and answers, I smugly sat with a smile and said, "Are we finished?" They stared at me and said after this mock process, "You will fail." I thought they were joking, and, after realizing they were serious, I asked them why. They informed me that I was answering the questions the way in which I would in the field, not as they are written in the "rule book."

The revered and loved Rabbi, the holy Ba'al Shem Tov, Master of the Good Name, reached the people by speaking in a language they understood, not as it is written in the book. When I went before the committee a couple of weeks later, I took the advice of my friends and peers and was granted my Board Certification. Sometimes the rules are spot on --- however, most of the time in real life situations, flexibility is called for in order to fill the spiritual gaps and desires for the people in our care and we have to tweak the rules. I am not advocating discarding the rulebook --- it is a good guide. When working in the field with my patients and their families, my responses, advice and blessings come from a space in my heart, rather than from the academic teachings of a book. I have to draw knowledge from what I've learned from the books and I blend this information with my own intuitive heart's teaching.

Chuppah Over The Nursing Home

IN MY TRAVELS AS A CHAPLAIN I visit many nursing homes and assisted living facilities. Some of these facilities offer kind-hearted, compassionate care to the residents; others, sadly, should be shut down due to their relative negligence in caring for those entrusted to their facility.

Our assisted living facilities and nursing homes house a great variety of individuals, some of whom suffer from dementia and some who are vibrant, but nevertheless require physical assistance. They are our mothers, our fathers, our sisters and brothers --- our family. These facilities are populated by those who have cared for us --- they taught us right from wrong; they gave us the tools to lead a quality life. Our elderly deserve the deepest respect and compassion at the end of their lives. The story you are about to read illustrates the best and happiest moments in a nursing home facility --- the way it can be.

MY MOTHER LIVED THE FINAL YEAR OF HER LIFE in a nursing home in Miami. Her body had failed her, but her mind stayed clear until the end. She had a great personality --- she was one of those bright souls who could always make anyone laugh. She always wanted to be helpful, no matter how frail she became.

The Jewish nursing home was located in a very poor neighborhood, known as "Little Haiti." After driving through the neighborhood and seeing the shacks and shanties, visitors arrived at the gate to the Home for the Aged. Traveling past the gate, one would reach a magnificently landscaped and quite pristine facility, admittedly in stark contrast to much about Little

Haiti. Beyond some of the buildings was the courtyard, where trees and flowers remained in bloom and comfortable benches were thoughtfully staged. Music played softly and the general atmosphere penetrated so completely one couldn't help but simply be relaxed.

One day my mother called me, saying she must speak with me right away --- she wanted me to visit her immediately about an important matter. Jackie and I left for her immediately. Upon our arrival she said that she wanted to introduce us to some of her best friends. She took our hands and escorted me through the hallways.

We were first introduced to her friend Ruth, who was a woman far past ninety. She wore fresh make-up and, like the surroundings, was elegant in her appearance. Her features revealed how beautiful she must have been as a younger woman. Indeed, she was still beautiful! Standing next to her was Henry, also well past ninety years of age. He had a head full of thick white hair. He was wearing shorts with high socks pulled to his knees. His wrinkled face told the story of surviving a hard life. His straight shoulders revealed an imposing dignity. Mom took my hand and introduced me as her son, "the rabbi." Jackie and I, though enjoying meeting these friends of my mother's, were still wondering why the urgency with which we were to visit. And then, all became clear.

My mother then proceeded to tell inform Ruth and Henry that, yes, I, her son, would be delighted to marry them. I stood somewhat shocked, probably quite rigid, frozen stiff, actually, and very surprised. I was cordial to both Ruth and Henry as I attempted to regain a social composure that suddenly felt so far off.

Ruth and Henry, taking turns, shared with me that they were truly in love and wanted to get married immediately. They both said they haven't felt a love like this since their late spouses died. They looked me in the eye and said, "We are old and are probably going to die soon. We want to join our souls." Henry took my arm, pulling me aside and assured me it was not only for the sex. He said "I mean, of course the sex will be good, but I really do love her. You can understand, son!" My main thought was, "*oy!*" followed immediately by, "*gevalt!*"

I assured them I would do some checking-in with their families and the administrative staff and that I would get back to them by the end of the week. I kissed my mother good-bye. As I left she gave me *the look*, and started toward the administrator's office. Leaving the grounds, we passed through the beautiful courtyard again. I looked up and pleaded, "*Ribono Shel Olam*…Master of the Universe! Please give me the wisdom to deal with this love story with blessings and with peace." I told Mom, I'd update her very soon.

I went to the administrative office and had a schmooze with the person in charge of the facility, who was aware of the situation. He said, shaking his head, "I can't see anything wrong with it, but you'd better check with the families first before we can proceed." I spoke to both families. They also thought it would be all right. I suggested we raise a *chuppah* in honor of the celebration, but not go through the State's formal legalities. I figured God overseeing and blessing this wedding was more important than the governor of Florida knowing about this.

All-in-all, it took about two weeks to have all the legal papers signed and, during this time, many faxes went back and forth. The date was finally set and these two were to be married in the warm months of a Miami winter. The children from both Ruth and Henry would fly to Miami from their homes out of state up north. I requested no press as I did not want a circus. The administrators of the facility wanted the press to cover the wedding, as it was good publicity. I wanted a holy space for these two. Jackie joined forces with my mom and they created a *ketubah* for Ruth and Henry to sign, also ordering flowers and decorations. She made sure the *chuppah* poles were ready and, finally, the big day arrived.

The families had arrived and were present for the signing of the *ketubah*. The courtyard was decorated with streamers and glitz. There was a beautiful *chuppah* supported by decorated poles. It was a flawless winter day in Florida --- the sun was shining and it was a near-perfect seventy-degrees. The path that the bride and groom would walk along was covered with red carpet and ended at the *chuppah*. A band played soft music and the sun danced through the blossoming trees. Henry appeared in his white tux with his shirt opened at the collar. His son and daughter escorted him. He said he did not need his walker, though it waited for him under the *chuppah*.

My mother was next - she was serving as the flower "girl." She proudly strutted down the isle sprinkling rose pedals on the red carpet. Then Ruth appeared, wearing a white dress and white shoes. She had a beautiful orchid on her shoulder and her hair was perfectly coiffed. She beamed as her sons escorted her to the *chuppah*. When they approached, their children along the aisles kissed them as they passed.

As I motioned for Ruth and Henry to join me, I glanced around the courtyard taking in the marvelous scene. The entire garden was lined with residents and staff, and the ones on the second and third floor that could not make it down to the courtyard ceremony leaned over the railing. A peace that I had never experienced at a nursing home or any assisted-living facility presided over all. These people were not only present to witness the wedding, they were there for hope --- hope for the past, the future and the present.

Henry and Ruth exchanged rings, and their children recited the *Sheva Brachot* blessing. Although this *kallah* and *chatan* were elderly, the energy we all experienced at that *chuppah* on this particular holy afternoon connected us back to our matriarchs and patriarchs. All who were witnessing this wedding were powerfully reminded that love is, truly, forever ageless. We all danced around them when the sixth blessing was recited. The nursing home staff provided lunch, and one staff member shared with my Jackie, "We pushed two beds together for them tonight."

As I drove away from the nursing home, I knew I learned that love is timeless, and we have to live each moment and treasure each day. Quietly, I thanked my Mom for including me in this great and wildly unexpected *mitzvah*.

I drove home following the wedding with a huge smile on my face. I honored both Ruth and Henry and, most of all, I honored my mother by fulfilling her wishes to make sure this wedding occurred. Driving, I also recalled the Orthodox rabbi who was the official clergy at the facility. He had placed his hand on my shoulder, following the ceremony, and said, "My beliefs did not allow me to create this ceremony. Thank you for doing this *mitzvah*."

Arising from this experience, assisting in the creation of a wedding ceremony that honored the love between two of our elders, I want to highlight an issue that has gone mostly unnoticed, but is now coming to fruition. Most of the elders living in assisted living facilities have lost their life partners and are very lonely. These individuals form alliances, which are at times sexual, loving connections. We live in a time of Viagra and other sexual enhancing medications. Some of our elders, previously sexual,, did not face the threat of AIDS and were unaware of STDs, sexually transmitted diseases. The staff at many of our nursing homes will not pass out condoms, which they believe will encourage the residents to engage in sexual promiscuity. So, they turn a blind eye --- sexuality is yet another issue, on top of all the other complex needs of their residents that they don't want to address and deal with. The use of condoms, in the minds of residents, was used only to prevent pregnancy, not STDs, because this was not in their reality or consciousness. Most, after all, only had one partner over the course of their life.

When love enters into the lives of the elderly, it can truly feel like a miracle. Love and sexuality, no matter what the age, go hand in hand. We must educate our elders to the fact they are not immune to the ravages of sexually transmitted diseases, if they are to celebrate an unforeseen loving relationship in their later years.

Different Strokes

Please, with your power of your great right hand,
Free the bound
Accept the song of your people
Empower us, purify us, Awesome One
— Rabbi Nechunya Ben Hakanah

IN OUR SOCIETY we tend to categorize or label someone who is different than us. There is a wide scope of mental illness and developmental disorders. Some people with an autism diagnoses are very high functioning and will lead a quality, useful life --- and some will not. All of them, however, are labeled autistic.

Some people suffer from bi-polar disorder. They, too, have a wide spectrum of ability and dis-ability. Some, with medications, are able to function in the real world and some, unfortunately, are not and may need to be hospitalized. We tend to label individuals with particular diagnoses so they fit into a particular group, rather than recognizing their individual, particular ways and levels of understanding. Placing individuals in need of spiritual care --- regardless of whatever varying degrees of mental illness or developmental disabilities they may be challenged with --- into one diagnostic group is archaic. Understanding and emotional perception varies widely from individual to individual. They, as all of us, function on different levels and we must learn to respect and engage individuals as such: as individuals.

AS PART OF MY RESIDENCY in Clinical Pastoral Education (CPE) I led services in the psychiatric unit at a hospital, the same unit I had shared about previously, above. My assignment was to lead the services, record them, and play them back to my supervisor and peer group of CPE students for their feedback. My assignment was to conduct a service that was to be interdenominational and multicultural. Upon entering the locked Psych unit, I was ushered into a room where all the patients were gathered. At the time I hadn't been informed there were four levels on the unit, each level comprised of people with minimal, moderate, intermediate and severe psychiatric issues. I was told that they could all be gathered together so I only would have one service to perform. This was the way it always was done. I thought of the consequences for the patient. How would a patient with a minimal mental problem be able to relate to a service for a patient with a severe problem and *vice versa*? I told them that for the benefit of the patient that I would hold four separate services and each service would be appropriate to the understanding of the four groups.

The attendant became irritated and told me that this was a radical change from how services were offered in the past. He did not want to take the extra time to separate the patients. I assured him I understood the difficulty to adjusting the routine, but that ultimately, for us to make the time to engage four services would lead to a more appropriate and meaningful service for all.

He became very agitated and threatened to report me and have me banned from the unit. It took time, however I was able to hold four completely different services quite successfully. I did not use a Unitarian Universalist book or any other composed worship service material previously prepared. I offered a service for each group that met their needs --- that they would not only comprehend, but would also be able to internalize, whatever their level of understanding, hopefully opening spiritual spaces within their hearts.

I've written previously about my days in the meat industry. During those years I remember crying as I saw the thousands of pigs being herded into the slaughter house. The pigs, too, were crying, as they somehow knew exactly what was happening. In my mind, it looked to me as though these holy challenged people were being robbed of their individuality and were being herded into a common area. I believe we, as clergy, we must remember this important lesson and, create a spiritual environment for the individual as well as the community at large. This is not easy and takes understanding and deep compassionate thought. I did not know where each person's challenged and wandering mind was, however, I did know that were not all functioning on the same level. I also knew that each person came into the world with a clear and holy soul and this was the place where I needed to make an effective connection.

The next morning I had to present a didactic and play my recording of the service for my CPE group and Supervisor. I relayed my experience in the unit, the challenges with adjusting the routine from one group to four, sharing with my supervisor there was no recording, and explained why I performed four separate services. My supervisor became livid and told me there needed to be a tape of one service so they could hear and analyze my ministry. I was told without reservation that I needed to go back again, offer services again and must make a recording of only one service. I stood my ground, knowing that although the system asked for only one service as a requirement of my training, I had to offer spiritual assistance on a deeper level. I offered to tape one of the services in order to satisfy the requirement. The supervisor, with the support of the feedback from my CPE peers, ultimately listened to me and agreed.

I returned the following week and led the one service. It was good for me to do this because I now had an accurate measure of how the one service was received rather than the four previous services. I went back to group and reported, and played my tape. The requirement had been met, however, I did not offer the people in the unit what they needed. I spoke about individual needs of people and how we, as clergy fill these needs. The group agreed with me and voted to offer only individual services from this point. In the following weeks a report came to our group that the director of this unit was very pleased with the transition and praised our group for changing the format. He stated that the new format led to harmony in the patient's actions during the week.

People with special needs have to be recognized at their individual level of need. When one has cancer we do not offer the same treatment that we give a heart patient. The medication and procedures vary. Nobody can really understand where the mental patient is on a spiritual plane - we can only speculate and offer therapy and medication through trial and error. This goal of the therapy is geared so that the patient can reach their highest attainable level. I believe if we also treat the spiritual level the patient will feel a sense of security that will enable them to live a more full life on a "day to day" living level

As a tribe, we all heard Moses give us the Ten Commandments at Sinai. We are taught that each one of us heard them a little differently. Each one of us heard them through our own history, our own DNA, our own hearts and we filter the message at our own level. I learned from this experience at the Psych Unit not to group people into one label, or into one service, but to celebrate each person's individuality, with all their holiness, with each one's dis-ability, and each one's shining heart.

"Thank You For Restoring My Soul"

The intention of my artwork is to enable all to open their heart and soul

- Jackie Olenick

I HAVE GIVEN MANY SERMONS and eulogies during the course of my career as a chaplain and as a rabbi. For my sermons I study text and attempt to see the inner meaning of the lesson so I can pass it along, that it be relevant in the modern world, for contemporary audiences. I want people to understand how the text applies in today's world and to our lives. When preparing a eulogy, I meet and speak with the family of the deceased who tell me about details of their loved ones life so I can choose appropriate stories to honor them with in the eulogy. Throughout the years, I have written thousands of words --- hopefully, all were meaningful and honorable.

People learn differently. Some need words, some music and some need a visual reference to learn a lesson or to come to a deep understanding leading to an open heart...

I WAS MAKING THE ROUNDS IN THE CARDIAC UNIT, one of my favorite units in the hospital because I can help people with understanding and compassion at a very intense level in natural and often times poignant ways. When people are in the cardiac unit they have usually suffered a heart attack or similarly related heart problem. Often times these patients have had their lives turned upside down and inside out. This usually comes as an unexpected shock to both the patient and their family members. In a split second their life style has changed. These challenges afford me the opportunity to work with them at a profound and intimate level. I attempt to embrace their fears, aligning myself with their experience as intense emotion and mind-states course through them, joining with their most vulnerable selves.

I often think of the passage from Psalm 90 when in the cardiac unit, which reads, "Teach us to treasure each day that we may open our hearts to your wisdom." Life is the ultimate gift from the Holy One of Blessing. We have our choice how we will treasure and use this bounty.

I entered a dark and dismal room. The shades were drawn, blocking the sun. The prevailing reverberation of the respiratory machine, *mantra*-like in its repetitive hum, provided the only audible sounds in the room.

Bill was lying very still in his bed. He was thin, and it seemed as though his searching eyes were larger than his face with prominent sunken and unshaven cheeks. His hair was disheveled and his general appearance was unkempt from long hours suffering through an invisible battle. He appeared defeated. To his right sitting on a drab blue chair was an elderly woman, Bill's wife, Joy. Her hair was neat, with the gray strands peeking through the red dye. She wore moderate make up that was neatly placed. She wore tasteful attire fitting for a senior citizen.

I introduced myself as the Chaplain. I was greeted warmly, and invited to sit. I learned that Bill's heart was tired and worn out. His cardiologist told him that his heart was functioning at a minimal level. The medical staff offered no hope of recovery. There was, apparently, no cure for him thus, he was told that he would be released from the hospital later in the day. The cardiologist delicately clarified for Bill and Joy that death could come at any time. Both Bill and Joy were recounting their life's story with me.

Joy said that they had been married for fifty years, but it didn't feel like enough time to leave Bill. She wanted more time to share more of life. Bill was brave as he spoke of his impending death. We spoke about end of life issues, from the practical matters to the spiritual ones. My duty as a Chaplain was to make sure that funeral arrangements were made and his house was put in order so his wife and family could go on with as little stress as possible. My bigger responsibility, however, was to listen deeply to Bill and his wife. Bill asked me if I knew what would happen to his soul and I responded, truthfully, that I did not know. I did tell him, however, that from our previous conversation and the good deeds he performed throughout his life, that his soul would be protected. This comforted him and Joy. Knowing he and Joy were Jewish, I asked about his Jewish practice. He said he never really practiced living as a Jew except for liking chicken soup, lox and bagels. We laughed together at the sweet superficiality in a moment with such pronounced heaviness. In my mind, I realized that the greater majority of Jewish patients I visit are of the "lox and bagel" variety of Jews. However, *they are Jews* and cling to our heritage no matter how the particular "observance" may manifest in their lives. He confided in me that he was now sorry that he was not more knowledgeable about the greater scope of Judaism as a religious tradition and wished he had been more active. I assured him that his life as a decent and gentle man was sufficient for God.

In my mind, I was taken back to the time when my son was at his college graduation ceremony. The Chancellor of the college gave an inspirational speech and I later found out that he had led a life of service and advocated social justice, making a change in the world for millions of people, as he was deeply involved in the Civil Rights movement. He had led an exemplary life. He was Jewish and yet not in any way religious. Upon returning home I spoke to a colleague who was a well-known rabbi in my community about this man's commitment to social justice, his charismatic personality and how he had so much influenced the world for the best. The rabbi's reply was disappointingly simplistic and narrow, "So, did he observe *Shabbat?*" This response meant to me that in this person's eyes, the rabbi's, the chancellor was diminished and not as good a person because he did not have an authentic religious practice. That telling and small minded reply allowed me to truthfully address Bill's concern about not following a religious, by the rule, path.

I asked if he would like me to recite the *Vidui* (the end of life Jewish confessional); He nodded, yes, it was time. I offered a prayer from my heart as well as the traditional end of life prayer:

"Holy One of Blessing, for anything Bill has done intentionally, or unintentionally, to harm anything or any person on this earth, forgive him.

*Ribono Shel Olam...*Master of the Universe, please summon Your holy angels to escort Bill when his soul returns to You; Michael at his right, Gabriel, at his left, Uriel before him, and Rafael behind him. Let them be joined by *Shekinah*, Your Holy Presence, so there is no fear walking through the 'valley of the shadow of death.' When his soul passes, let him be greeted by familiar faces, and the people with whom he feels comfort and love that have left the world before him."

"Let Joy *know* that death cannot take away the love and bond they share. Let her realize that their souls are braided like a *challah* and they will be braided for life-beyond-life. Bless her with strength and courage to embrace these braids as she walks life's path. Amen."

It was time for me to exit. Bill grabbed my hand and said, "Wait, there is one prayer that I have said since I was a little kid. My grandfather taught it to me. I say it every day and I don't even know the meaning." I asked him to say the prayer. He proudly recited:

Modeh ani l'fanacha, melech chai v'kayam,
Shehechezarta b'nishmati b'chemlah,

Rabbah emunatecha. Amen.

I gratefully thank You, Living God,
for compassionately returning my soul to me, daily,
--- thank You for this trust. Amen.

This is the Morning Prayer that we offer as thanks for restoring our soul anew, each day. We spoke of how it felt to be so thankful for all the years that the soul was restored, daily, after its incredible journey's into the night, venturing through the universe to "learn Torah." We are taught that as we sleep our soul has the freedom to travel in the Universe and complete missions necessary for its evolution. We sometimes recall these universal visits as dreams, and sometimes as *deja vu*. Of course, we don't really know where our soul travels, but not being wholly bound by our body it therefore has total movement. We do, however, welcome it back when we awaken each day with this prayer.

I thought how ironic that this is the prayer he is familiar with at this time when his soul is preparing to leave and not return. Bill was connecting to a prayer he learned as a child from his beloved grandfather who, I believe, will greet him when his soul no longer returns to earth. On a soul level, this is an exquisite connection of "from generation to generation".

As I exited the room I felt that on some level I had offered this family meaningful spiritual care, however I didn't feel we connected quite as deeply as is sometimes the case. I did not fill the space of anticipated emptiness they were experiencing. Bill and Joy did not have experience with "soul" talk. This was something new and inaccessible for them. I had to make a connection they could understand on another level.

My wife, Jackie, is an artist who creates visual interpretations of her inner visions of Torah and its teachings. Upon arriving home, I went into our kitchen for a drink of water. Before me was one of Jackie's illuminated paintings; it was the *"Modeh ani."*

With Jackie's encouragement, I brought this painting to the hospital later that day, presenting it to Bill and Joy. I could tell how important it was for them to have an image, embodied, of this prayer.

My heart dictated this action, and I have learned that it is this subtle intuition of the heart that we must cultivate being sensitive to, listening to it's quiet yet direct inspiration, acting upon such beautiful clarity. I now felt that I connected with them more wholly and profoundly.

Bill was, in fact, released and as it would turn out, I didn't hear from him again. About five weeks later, however, I received a letter from Joy:

> *Dear Rabbi Leon,*
>
> *I don't know if you remember Bill and me: You visited us in the hospital and brought us one of your wife's pictures, the one with the "Modeh Ani" prayer.*
>
> *Bill died last week. He was in such anguish, confined to bed and denied even minimal movement. I believe death may have been a blessing.*
>
> *The reason for this letter was to thank you. The last weeks of Bill's life were like a honeymoon for us. We hung the picture of the blessing you gave us where we could view it, and each morning I cuddled up to Bill as he recited the "Modeh ani." We held each other tightly, and understood what it meant to be grateful for restoring life and we felt our love renewed. We were like newlyweds.*
>
> *I will continue to look at the picture each morning as I remember my Bill and recite his prayer.*
>
> *Sincerely,*
>
> *Joy*

Harkening back to my time with them, I remembered that as I exited Bill's hospital room, I was spiritually pushed --- encouraged to act from a subtle place --- to do something physical, rather than just being present and offering explanations of the soul. They needed something physical --- something they could touch and see for them to move forward. My connection to this couple was not in my current pastoral toolbox, so to speak. I added a tangible tool in the form of artwork to the toolbox. If I did not recognize their immediate need, I would haven't have aided in their final "together-ing" they so intimately shared the last few weeks. The picture supported them in the process of connecting and, thus, more fully letting go, peacefully and yet *in* Love. The lesson to listen to more fully to the intuition of the heart was a good and poignant lesson for me.

*   *   *

As a spiritual counselor, I am trained to listen. Although tempted to counsel with words, sometimes a simple visualization is better able to fulfill the needs of the patients and families. Through deep listening, I am able to understand the needs of the patient --- at whatever level they can integrate into their lives. I attempt to keep my ego in check and not offer a long discourse so that the words and message, in which no one, but me, would absorb. Sometimes, simple is best.

My Love Is Down The Street

Many waters cannot quench love, neither can floods drown it.

- Song of Songs 8:7

WE ARE TAUGHT, both as youngsters and adults, about boundaries, limits and rules. Sometimes these need expansion when circumstances dictate. People take chances and cross boundaries, sometimes for negative and sometimes for positive reasons or intentions. We recall stories from Shakespeare, "Romeo and Juliet," or from Broadway, "West Side Story," or "South Pacific" where boundaries were crossed in the name of love. Everyday people --- those of us who think of ourselves as having ordinary lives --- find ourselves in a position of crossing boundaries for love. Love makes boundaries appear infinite.

RUTH HAD HAIR AS WHITE AND SPOTLESS AS THE FRESH SNOW that now covered the ground outside of the hospital. Her room was decorated with pictures of her family. In one photograph I saw her husband of sixty-years standing tall, holding her hand and smiling when they were much younger. Her children, grandchildren and great-grandchildren looked happy and were dressed beautifully in the spring-time, pastel hued scene. Cards from family and friends were taped to the wall. The cards handmade and written with crayon by her great-grandchildren stood out prominently amidst the other loving décor and it appeared she was a long-time resident of this particular hospital room.

Ruth was quiet, aware and serene. As I approached her she greeted me

119

with a warm smile, conveying an inner peace. Her presence was that of a matriarch who had witnessed a great deal of life. Anyone who is the matriarch of a large family lives through big and small dramas; births of children, their children, and their children; illness; death; financial ups and downs and day-to-day events we call life.

I learned Ruth entered the hospital about four weeks earlier for hip replacement surgery. This was typically a simple procedure, with individuals normally released from the hospital a few days after surgery. However, after her surgery Ruth suffered a life-threatening infection. She had been quite near death, however, with swift intervention by the medical team she was now recovering. When we met she was restricted to the bed while the antibiotics healed her body.

I sat down next to her and introduced myself. She took my hand and held it very tightly. "Can you help me?" she asked. Tears began to flow from her full brown eyes. She continued, "My husband, Milton, is very ill. He was fine when I entered the hospital. He said he would be present to care for me when I returned home. Last week, however, he stopped visiting. Immediately I knew something was not right. My family tried to hide his problem from me, however I recently found out that he suffered a severe stroke and is now very ill. My children finally told me that the stroke was serious and he will not survive. I must see him!"

"We have shared our bed for 60 years. We have laughed, loved and argued...I know life is short and can end anytime, however he cannot go without me holding his hand, kissing him and hearing me say, 'I love you,' at least one more time. He is in the hospital down the street and they say I am too ill to visit him..."

Her tears intensified. "Please help me get to Milton and say goodbye to him, my love."

She then told me some stories of their life together and invited me into their life-long adventure. After spending the afternoon with her and hearing her stories, I told her I would investigate and see what I could do, however I couldn't promise anything at the time. I did promise, however, to visit Milton myself and report back to Ruth

After leaving the room I further investigated the reality of the situation. I discovered that Milton was, indeed, at a hospital about ten miles away. I called the hospital and spoke to the Director of Nursing. She told me that Milton was terminally suffering from the stroke and was on life support. She said end of life decisions would have to be made by the family. After hanging up the phone I followed up with the Director of Nursing at the hospital where I was working and where Ruth was currently residing. I was told it was not possible for Ruth to travel to Milton due to the high cost of paying a registered nurse who would have to accompany her, as well as the ambulance transport. This was, indeed, potentially very expensive. I called her family and they shared with me they could not afford to make Ruth's request to travel to Milton between hospitals happen.

I pondered what there was to do. I thought of the importance of being with the ones we love prior to death. I thought of Jacob, in the Torah, summoning Joseph's sons, Menasha and Ephraim, prior to his death in order to bless them. I knew in my heart that in order for Ruth to have closure, and Milton to have the peace to leave the world, they must be together, as they were daily for the last 60 years of their lives.

I decided to make some inquiries of my own and, if necessary, to request some favors on behalf of these two. I called the ambulance company and spoke to the director. I informed him of the situation. He hesitated and there was silence on the other end for a few minutes. He started speaking with a broken voice. He told me that he lost his wife and was not able to be with her when she died and now he could help someone else be with their loved one. He offered to provide the ambulance at no cost. I then spoke to some of the nurses staffing both hospitals and the related departments.

Most of the nurses at the hospital work 12-hour shifts and they are exhausted afterward, wanting to return home to their own families rather than put in overtime hours, let alone, unpaid. They, too, saw the importance of saying farewell to a loved one and volunteered to accompany Ruth after their shift. Because Ruth was a patient in the hospital now for weeks, the staff had grown to love her and wanted to help her see her husband. I was hoping that one nurse would volunteer, however, several nurses jumped at the opportunity to do this *mitzvah* and honor Ruth. Now that all was in place, I had to receive the clearance of the hospital administration, strictly for administrative and insurance purposes, and have the family sign a waiver. This was all quite swiftly and, miraculously accomplished; it felt like these efforts were being blessed by a grace and approval from above.

I underestimated my co-workers willingness, even given this particular situation. I did not have to call in *any* favors. All were quite anxious to help in their respective ways.

Once Ruth was in the ambulance, we proceeded to the hospital down the street where Milton remained. As we drove I did my best to prepare her so she would not be quite as shocked to see Milton on life support. At the hospital, I went ahead to Milton, making sure he was presentable, and then Ruth was wheeled to his side.

She took his hand and spoke very softly to him as I excused myself for them to have the privacy they so needed. As I left I assured her that he is able to hear every word she is saying, although he cannot respond.

After about 30 minutes I reentered the Intensive Care Unit. She was still holding his hand, tears flowing as she gently sang loving songs to him. It was if I had entered holy ground, witnessing the comforting song of an angel to a soul in need. Shortly thereafter, it was time to leave.

I recited the *vidui* for Milton. As Ruth kissed him, her tears fell to his cheeks and it was as if their tears were of one source. We left and returned Ruth to her hospital. After she was settled back in her room, with her family awaiting her arrival, the nurse and driver thanked me for inviting them to be part of this difficult and yet beautiful *mitzvah*.

Milton was taken off life support and died shortly thereafter. I officiated his funeral service where I spoke directly to Milton's soul, before all those gathered, that Ruth was with him. I addressed Milton, that as they stood under the *chuppah* together, they were together even now, and forever more.

Sadly, Ruth was unable to attend the funeral due to her condition. After the service I went to the hospital, cut the black ribbon on her nightgown, which signified a mourner, and we recited the *kaddish*. I again assured Ruth that each time she recites the *kaddish* she is sending sparks of light directly to Milton's soul. I again offered her a prayer for healing and then left her alone to mourn her love.

So many of the patients I am privileged to be with have relatives living in far away cities. Their personal lives, jobs and families do not allow them to cross the borders of their day-to-day lives as frequently as they wish. Milton was only ten miles away from Ruth, however, for her it may as well have been a thousand miles. Thanks to modern technology we now have numerous means of instant communication at our disposal, even face-to-face. With permission from families and functioning within the privacy rules of HIPPA, I use my phone and tablet to aid in the communication of clients out of physical range with a loved one. Ruth's tears could not have fallen on Milton's cheeks with simply a phone or the like, so this technique is not perfect. However, it does afford contact, when contact seems impossible. I was so touched by the support of the health care workers, ambulance, hospital administration; all those involved in making Ruth's wish possible. Sometimes all we have to do is ask.

Anorexia, Fat, Thin & In-Between

And you shall eat, and be satisfied, and bless.

- Deuteronomy 8:10

"MIRROR, MIRROR ON THE WALL, who's the thinnest of them all?" This quote, this idea, like the fashion industry in general, permeates every aspect of modern culture; gigantic billboards with skinny women, television advertisements blaring every conceivable diet method, radio advertisements offering special deals for the latest diet fad, and even internet emails sending advertising featuring spa treatments, cellulite treatments and highlighting fashions for "skinny" jeans, flimsy tops, sexy revealing underwear ads and on and on. Of course, fashion models wear these designs. We are barraged with never ending messages that announce being skinny is good, fashionable and beautiful.

Most women I know do not look like these models and are, in fact, truly beautiful. In an attempt to live up to this expectation, many women choose bulimia or anorexia as an antidote to their self-image fears. Whether they look perfect and beautiful or not, in their eyes, they see themselves as overweight, or at least not meeting the prescribed fashion code. Anorexia and bulimia are a disease maybe caused by the subliminal messages via the advertising. It gets into the heads and psyches of young women starting them on the downward path of an eating disorder. Initially it is typically is a psychological issue, but it spirals into a deadly psychophysical disease. It becomes the "drug of choice" and the habit is extremely difficult to break. The body withers, the teeth become rotted, lack of nourishment causes the internal organs to fail, and the passion to lead a healthy lifestyle fades away. There is no magic pill for this disorder. Oftentimes eating disorders are left undiagnosed because early on there is no physical sign that can be discerned by loved ones. It is a silent killer and we are hesitant, even if we recognize signs, to intervene. We don't step forward, perhaps because we are angry with our loved one, and/or our denial that our daughter is not perfect --- as we define perfection in a woman. We are all created in God's image and we've been given the holy gift of food. We must teach our children to eat respectfully and also that they, too, are created in the image of God.

I HAVE STRUGGLED WITH WEIGHT ISSUES all my adult life. Whenever I gain weight it affects my mood. When I feel overweight I'm ashamed to tuck my shirt in, I feel unattractive and become overly conscious of being looked at. When I feel like this, my mind cruelly takes over, the broken-record in my mind stuck in a loop, to the words, "I feel fat, I appear fat, I am fat." However, when I am more balanced, eat right and exercise regularly, working the weight off, I feel confident again. At this time I feel whole, more like myself and confident in the world.

I usually don't weigh myself; I can tell by the way my clothes fit whether or not I'm where I want my body to be. Keeping myself on schedule with physical fitness that is comfortable remains a struggle that I live with, daily.

I was in a psychiatric unit of a major hospital at one of the finest educational institutions in our country. On my rounds, I visited a young woman. Prior to my visit, I reviewed Joan's chart. She was anorexic and was admitted from the regular hospital after being treated, near death medical episode caused by malnutrition. She was very attractive. Her cheekbones were prominent, although her cheeks were sunken. Her eyes were rimmed with dark circles masking their full beauty. Joan was about twenty years old, had the body of a prototypical model, and attended a prestigious college with a full scholastic scholarship.

When I first meet a patient, because I haven't yet had the opportunity to get to know them at all, I choose to engage in small talk as a way of introduction, enabling me to ease into the real issues at hand. Although I had already reviewed her chart and knew why she was hospitalized, I wanted to hear from Joan in her own words. When a patient, in their own words, reveals their diagnoses or habit or problem, it validates to them the reality of their situation. I asked her why she was here and she said directly, and very nonchalantly, "I'm anorexic." I asked what this meant to her. Joan said, "I am too fat. I have to protect my appearance so I binge eat and then force myself to throw up after eating." Her understanding of the disease impressed me --- she appeared to know of all the factors of anorexia and intellectually understand the possible consequences. This admission raised a concern to me that her disease was acceptable for her existence.

"It's all right," she replied. "I do eat, you know." We spoke about eating and receiving the necessary nourishment for the body to function. Our discussion went around in fairly predictable circles. I looked her in the eyes and sharply said, "Do me a favor and cut the 'cutesy' crap. I grew up on the streets of Philadelphia, and have been trained as a professional Chaplain."

I spoke to her in this tone so that she clearly would know, because of my "street" background, that I was savvy to her trying to manipulate and seduce me. I knew she wanted me as yet another partner in enabling her to continue her deadly behavior. Joan paused for a few minutes, looked at me and began to cry.

"I can't help it! I binge and throw up! I don't know why I do it. I wish I could stop." She was sobbing, tears ruining her makeup, giving the outward appearance of dark blotches on her beautiful face --- her mask was being removed. I believe she realized that I was not going anywhere until she was honest with me and that it would be impossible to fool me, as she had others.

"I know the psychologists, psychiatrists and doctors are working with you, to best address the physical and psychological roots of this cruel disease. Share with me a bit about how you *feel* inside your *soul*."

"I want to be whole and make a difference in the world," she said as I handed her tissues to dry her eyes. "I know I will be okay if they would only leave me alone." I encouraged her to go on. "My family thinks I have to be perfect. I am their 'perfect child.' I have a full scholarship, I must be perfect in school, perfect in sports, perfect in my looks...I am an object that they can brag about to family, neighbors and friends. I am *not* perfect! *Nobody* is perfect and I only want to be *me*!"

I took her hand, "How do *you* see yourself? How do you think God sees you?" She looked up, "I see myself as fat and ugly and I'm sure God sees me the same." I responded with a question for her to consider, rather than offering more fuel for her resistance to connecting with me, "Let me ask you something: How do you think God sees any of the creatures placed on earth? Do you believe that you and they are judged by appearance? You have heard the cliché, 'beauty is in the eyes of the beholder.' Well, I want to tell you that all of God's creations are beautiful in God's 'eyes,' and we all have a mission, a *responsibility* to lead happy, healthy lives." The smile she met me with was a nervous, but trusting smile. Some of the barriers between us were crumbling as we slowly connected. "I really want to help you to be in touch with your-self, and I am not sure how to accomplish this. You have me stumped."

I was, in fact, mystified. It felt, in some ways, that I had met my match as a chaplain, i.e., it was obvious she needed help and, from a certain vantage wanted help, but fitting through the door, so to speak...I had to be smaller to fit through the crack. On one hand, she knew what had to be done for her growth and wellbeing, yet on the other hand she would not accept the responsibility for her part. Granted, I could not "fix" her as we are unable to "fix" anybody. All I could do was to listen with compassion and attempt to spark a spiritual flame that would ignite her from the inside out, and open a path for her to connect with her precious soul..

She said, "You could pray for me." Immediately I took her hand and I prayed for her. My blessing to Joan was simple:

"Holy One of Blessing, give Joan the strength to see herself as You see her. Her mission in life has just begun and her offerings will send sparks to you and the world. Heal her body, mind and spirit and enable her to see the gift of food, which You have provided as her sustenance. Grant her the strength to care for her body as nature cares for our earth"

It was a deep but short prayer intending to let her see her inner beauty, and accept her own self-worth. I gave her a hug and began to leave the room. She asked me to wait.

"There is something else you can do for me. My father is coming this afternoon to bring me back to Ohio for therapy. I am taking three months off from school and will go home and really try to break this pattern. They will not let me out of here until my father comes. Will you go to my dorm room? Hidden under my mattress and in my pillowcase and in my drawer are candy bars and other junk food. Will you remove these for me before he comes, so he will not see these?"

I knew that people who suffered from anorexia loved to stock pile junk food, binge and then vomit. I shared with her, no, I could not. I did offer, however, to accompany her and her father to the dorm and stay there while they packed her belongings. "But he will see!" as she pleaded her case further. I looked at her and shared it was important to see under the bed, in her personal belongings, in every corner of her dorm room, and watch as she packed her bags. She, her father and I needed to witness the recovery of all this food, as it was evidence as to the magnitude of her addiction.

Her father arrived a few hours later. He signed the necessary papers for her release and was given sealed charts for her doctor to follow up, once back in Ohio. He approached his daughter with great compassion and love. She fell into his arms and he was reassuring her all would be fine. She said, "Why don't you get the car and I will throw my stuff in a bag and meet you. That way we will save time." He thought that was a good idea. From my interaction with Joan, I realized that Daddy saw her as his perfect little girl. I felt deep down he knew what would be found in Joan's room. I felt he had to witness it in order for Joan's problem to become a reality. If he could not face the fact that his little girl was suffering from anorexia, how could he possibly help her back home in Ohio.

She was attempting to manipulate the situation in her favor. I stepped in, introduced myself and said, "I promised Joan I would keep her company while she packed. Why don't we all go to the dorm together?" She glared at me with half closed eyes. I could tell, at the moment, she felt betrayed by me, that I was disclosing her secret. Entering the dorm room I did not utter a word. Sometimes words are not appropriate. I did however see the anguish on her father's face as more and more junk food appeared from beneath sheets, stuffed in drawers and other hidden away spots. I believe he was angry with me for making him face the true magnitude of Joan's disease. He now also had to face reality, and explore his soul. His perfect little girl was not perfect and desperately needed his help, not his usual lavish compliments regarding his daughter's perfection. His daughter did not need to be coddled --- she needed tough therapy to regain her life.

They pulled away without saying goodbye to me. They were both angry with me. I realized that, as a Chaplain, my job is to help repair the wounded spirit, however my toolbox does not contain the instruments to fix the wounded body. I hoped that I was able to make a connection for this father and daughter between their wounded spirits and her wounded body.

I did know, however, as long as he paraded Joan as the perfect child, she would not recover.

As parents, we all want perfect children. We want them to be the most beautiful, the most intelligent, the greatest athlete --- no "flaws" in *our* family!

Our DNA dictates, as parents, that we are entitled to bragging rights. We make our children believe they are the center of the universe. We lavish them with praise --- we ignore bad behavior because we don't want to damage their fragile psyche. We expect highest grades, entrance into the best colleges, and we make them feel they must best, the brightest, the best looking. All these wishes of ours instill the same subliminal messages that appear in the advertising industry. As parents, we want our children to have a better life than we have had. However, I also know that children must learn through their own mistakes, as I have learned through mine. We pray and worry that they don't engage in risky behavior that places them in a trajectory of a ruined life.

Our children know that as parents, we do provide safety nets. But, I will not ignore self-destructive habits. These will be noticed and addressed. When my children were teenagers, I made them promise that if they were at a party and drinking (even though we didn't give them permission to underage drink), that they would not attempt to drive home. They knew they could call us, would not be yelled at, and they would be safely driven home by their parents. They knew we would visit the situation the next day in a calm manner.

During my visit with Joan, as shared above, her anorexic condition was obvious. During her fathers visiting time with Joan, it was evident that he was in denial of his daughter's disorder, obstructing Joan's pathway to regaining her health. As parents, we can't put the unrealistic pressure of flawlessness on our children forcing them into addictions, into eating disorders, into self-destructive behavior that could end up lethal in the name of having raised a perfect child. No one is perfect. We all have flaws. Through the difficult challenge of recognizing and accepting our own shortcomings, we must learn not to project them on to our children. From this understanding we are able to go forward and resume life fully, knowing that our next challenge will not be our last.

Choose Life

This day I call the heavens and the earth as witnesses against you that I have set before you life and death, blessings and curses [...] children may live.

- Deuteronomy 30:19

ALMOST DAILY WE READ ABOUT PEOPLE attempting, or, in fact, committing suicide. A great many of these fatalities are teenagers who do not see a future. Many people who are having struggles have lost their loved ones, their jobs or homes in the economy collapse, or some even have lost a beloved pet. A record number of suicides or attempts at suicide are caused by grief, and a fear of the unknown. Many people who are having thoughts of suicide are in a deep pathological depression. Certain attempts are planned very carefully, and some are impulsive. They all are a cry for help and understanding. Their silent screams call out, "listen to me!" Unfortunately, *tragically*, the person feels so incomplete they believe suicide is their only choice.

Through much of our popular media, such as books and movies, which tell stories of suicide, the sequence ends and the actors move on to another movie with another plot. In real life, the end of a life is final.

JIM, A GOOD-LOOKING MAN, was recuperating from a serious surgery. He had a very lengthy illness and was finally on the path to health. Jim was thirty-five years old, stood about six feet tall with thick black wavy hair and the kind of face that told me that he was very attractive before his illness. I introduced myself and he invited me sit with him.

After some reluctance, he started sharing his story with me. he debilitating condition he was suffering from was overbearing, lasting a year-and-one-half. During this time he lost everything. "My fiancé left me; the business I started went bankrupt. Hell, the bank would have repossessed my home if my brother had not taken over the payments." He was convinced that he was left with nothing. His face went rigid and his voice grew bitter, "I am going to be released in a few days."

I declared "That is great news, Jim, you are well and, as your body becomes stronger, you can rebuild your life." Then the tone in his voice grew even more ominous and he whispered, "I am going home, and when I get there I am getting my gun, placing it my mouth and killing myself. My life is over! I just don't see the point of getting stronger again." I stopped him. "Jim, I must inform you, before you say more, by law I am required to report anyone planning harm to themselves, or any one else, to the appropriate authority. If you wish to continue, I will listen, but I need you to understand this point. Do you understand?" He nodded yes, and continued.

"What do I have to live for? I lost everything I had, everything I worked for and the only woman I ever loved, ditched me. I am nowhere! I am nothing!" I took his hand and held it as his voice quivered and broke. He wept and fell into my arms. About a half hour passed before another word was uttered. The silence wasn't uncomfortable and even seemed helpful for him.

I believe that a great many of us are afraid of silence. I believe it is a gift. Silence allows us the inner time to organize our thoughts, and our perspective. If we let it, silence lets us transcend our minute-to-minute panic and permits us to transcend our narrow points of view. Whenever I teach, speak or facilitate a life cycle service, I allow space for silence. When officiating at a funeral service, I ask people to close their eyes, sit in silence and ask them to recall the first thing that comes to mind in a time they shared with the deceased. I instruct them, not to think, but to capture the first image that comes into their hearts. I know, for some, this is uncomfortable, however for most, they open their eyes and wipe away the tears of memory. Many have said to me they felt they have sent a message to their loved one and thanked me for allowing those moments of silence.

Jim didn't share his thoughts during this time of silence, however, from his demeanor I knew his thinking had shifted to a different perspective. At that point, I was able to speak to him about the blessing of life itself. Because it was clear to me that some light was now visible in his eyes, I felt he was able to feel the blessing of life. My teacher Reb Shlomo Carlebach taught me that the heart that is completely whole is the heart which has been broken. We all possess an inner strength that creates a path to wholeness. This path always exists. Our task is to follow it, and find it again when we wander away. "I know your past has been devastatingly challenging and you are tired of fighting against what appears an inherently cruel world, but a positive future may be in your sight. Your body has healed, although your heart and soul have not. Your brother saved your house so you have shelter. You have family support and your chances for body, mind and financial recovery are all possible. Jim, jump into life." Jim was listening intently and by his facial expressions, I knew he was not only listening, but hearing and internalizing.

I took a breath and told him "Jim, you know I have to report this and I am not allowed at this point to leave you alone, so what would you like me to do? Do you really wish to die? I can contact the social worker or the charge nurse to admit you to psychiatric care. It is your choice."

Jim pronounced that he would admit himself. He whispered that he wanted to die, but also wanted to live. He was confused. He told me he was living this non-life for so long --- unable to move, unable to use his body ---

that he lost sight of what it really is to live a life. I smiled and held him until those who could best support him arrived. Prior to his leaving I told him, "Be a blessing, Jim --- choose life."

I did not follow Jim's progress in the Psychiatric Unit, or have any contact with him following his release. I do not know if he put his life together, chose life, or not. Like Jim, most of us have disappointments and challenges that seem, at the moment, insurmountable; And, some of them are, in fact, not fixable. A love that is lost, a failed business that cannot be recovered, a terminal diagnoses are just some of the events that catapult us into a downward spiral. I don't possess the cure for recovery regarding life's losses. I do know that by sharing our concerns, feelings with trusted people who are able to listen and understand, that we may find a way to lift ourselves out of a scary void and into the blessing of life.

This story above addressed the epidemic of suicide, which destroys not only the life of the victim, but the lives of people who love us, whether we acknowledge this love or not, as well as future generations which have the toxic shadow of a suicidal family member cast upon them. Suicide does not solve any of life's problems.

I bless you, the reader, to recognize signs of potential suicide victims and attempt to be present for them, as well as try your best to get them the professional help they need. The Baker Act is a national law put into place, in which the person threating his or her own life is placed in a Psychiatric Unit for 72 hours. This short hiatus will allow the potential suicide the time to "cool down" and assess their actions. "Be a blessing, choose life."

The School Bus

IF WE HAVE BEEN BLESSED to have children, nothing is more important to us than their well-being. For those who are not parents, we have nieces, nephews, neighbors or children of friends that we cherish. Whatever the case, we strive to protect them, keep them safe so that they will grow to adulthood, and with our guidance, lead quality lives.

When I enter my car, my first act, like many of us, is to buckle my seat belt. In an airplane, the announcement tells us to fasten our seatbelts. At the time of this story, and I believe, in many of our cities today, seat belts are not required on our school busses. Several years ago one of the congressional delegates from my district was giving a speech at a local event. Following the event I was able to speak to him, shake his hand, and I asked him about my concern for not having seat belts on public school busses. He answered that he believed they should be there, however, the funds to install seat belts on each school bus are not available, they are "not in the budget" I was told. During our conversation, I explained that many times while riding in my car behind a school bus I could see the children jumping up and down --- clearly not strapped in. The law is explicit. We will receive a ticket if we don't buckle our seat belt in our car. The airplane won't leave until passengers are secured. However, the safety of our vulnerable, precious children is ignored because of dollars and cents.

WE TAKE CERTAIN RESPONSIBILITIES FOR GRANTED, and feel we do not have to place too much energy in them, as they are routine. One of these is preparing our children for school. We feed them breakfast, make sure they are clean and dressed and send them off to school. We sometimes escort them to the bus stop and wait until the school bus arrives to wave and tell them to have a good day. Usually at this time we are able to take a deep breath and continue with our morning routine, knowing they are safe.

It was a beautiful fall day in Minnesota. We encouraged our children to wear a light sweater to school. I was at the hospital making routine rounds when the pager went off, and I was summoned to the Emergency Room. This, at the time, did not faze me, so to speak, as it was quite normal for me to visit the E.R. sometimes several times throughout one day.

Walking down the hallway, I was greeted by several of my colleagues who were also called to the E.R. as well. We look at one another hoping one of us could clarify what was happening for the rest. Was this some kind of drill? We were escorted to a private meeting room where we found *all* the chaplains and social workers on duty also present. The hospital Chief Executive Officer came in with his press secretary and the hospital legal counsel. He was clearly in a somber mood. As he stood before us the stress in his face and actions told us there was a problem. His body was rigid as he approached the podium.

He addressed us, "A school bus carrying fifteen elementary school children was just involved in a serious accident. The bus went off the road and rolled over several times. The children are in route here now: some will arrive via helicopter, some via ambulance. We do not have details on individual conditions. The parents were notified and are also in route. As each family arrives you are to line up and each take a family. You are to stay with this family during triage informing them of the condition of their children, and comfort them, offering anything they need.

No parent will be allowed to enter the E.R., as it will be far too busy, so you must explain that you are the contact, interfacing between them and the E.R. staff. You can enter the E.R. as many times as is helpful to get updated reports. As each child is addressed and moved from the E.R. you will be able to escort the family to the bedside of their child. You will stay with the family full-time and not permit them to wander past the individual room. In the event the child dies, you will escort the family to a private room and inform them of the death. Offer your care. If the media asks you questions, you will not address them. Point them to the media room that is presently being set up to receive the press. The families will arrive soon. As they do, take one family and remain with them until you have an update on their child."

"Let us offer a prayer that all the children survive, and we are able to comfort and assist the family." The prayer was led by one of my fellow chaplains.

I went to the lobby and waited, as instructed. Sitting by myself in a corner of the lobby, I felt fear and tension forming and taking over my body. Usually, when all us chaplains are together we talk, joke around a bit and catch up with one another. Today as we sat together the room was silent and heavy. I wondered, "What family will I serve? Will this child survive? Would their injury cause permanent damage, God forbid?!"

"God, be with me now as I care for this as of yet unknown child and family. Let Your compassion and words come through me, comforting them. May all the children survive this terrible accident and be able to lead long lives filled with Your Blessed Energy and help further create a peaceful world." I concluded chanted a blessing that I use in an emergency situation such as this. The prayer is called "*Anna b'koach*" --- I think of this as my "911" prayer.

As I finished chanting, the doors flung opened. The press and television news teams arrived *en masse* at the same time families were being ushered into the hospital. As the families arrived in the front with the press the ambulances were arriving via the back E.R. doors. The sounds of the helicopter blades whisking through the air were in the background.

I have long related to chaos in a positive manner. The Torah teaches us, "the world was created from Chaos, and it was good." For me, chaos allows me to sharpen my thought pattern and reaction ability. When performing my duties as a chaplain, I do not fear chaos. The minutes passed quickly and I was up; I was to serve the next family through the doors before me.

The sliding door rolled to its side and a man and woman entered. The man, in his early forties, wore work overalls that were dirty from working all morning. He was a burley, stout man and spoke in a deep, bass voice. Looking into his eyes, all two-hundred-plus-pounds of him were beseeching me, "where is my little girl?!"

The woman, dressed in a housecoat, was petite, but she was screaming, "Where is Jane?! I want to see my Jane!" Her screams were met with even more screams and the panic of other families. Pandemonium had, indeed, taken over the emergency room. Fear had overcome order and the screams were being engulfed into the greater cosmos, directed to the Holy One, though at this point we were confined to a room in the E.R.

I introduced myself as the Chaplain and took the two parents to a corner of the room. I asked their name and the last name of Jane. I did not attempt to comfort them as this was a moment beyond comfort. I told them to remain where they were and I would inquire whether Jane had arrived. They agreed and I went to the back of the emergency room. Doctors and nurses were scurrying about, yelling orders to one another as they administered to the patients; again, more bedlam. It was difficult to ask anyone to pause for information so I went to the triage desk and glanced at the names and room assignments. Jane's name did not appear. I thought, "this could be a blessing or a curse, God forbid." I hoped it was a blessing, implying that her injuries were not too severe and she could wait; I feared a curse because she may have died at the scene. At this time I did not know which one was correct.

I returned to the family, informing them she had not yet arrived. We spoke cordially, simply trying to remain composed amidst the devastating and frenzied scene. As it would turn out, these parents had older children, but Jane was their unexpected "gift from God" in their later years. I excused myself again to re-enter the E.R. to see if Jane had arrived. Indeed, this time, checking the triage list, I discovered Jane was in E.R. room number six. I raced to the room to discover a curly blond hair little girl crying from pain inflicted by this terrible event.

Jane couldn't have weighed more than eighty pounds. Her jeans and T-shirt were torn and she had scuffmarks on her hands and face. I approached her and took her hand as I wiped the tears from her cheeks. "Hi sweetie, my name is Leon. Your mommy and daddy are outside and they will see you soon." She looked into my eyes and continued to cry. I did not want to go and report to the parents just yet, as I had no facts to share with them. I had no idea what extent her injuries were. I sat next to her stroking her hand and wiping away tears until a doctor entered.

"Take her to get x-rays," was the order I overheard. I asked the doctor for an initial report I may present to the parents. The doctor said she was definitely suffering from a broken arm and leg. She had a concussion and they wanted a CAT-scan to determine if there was any brain damage and/or internal bleeding. I exited the room and went to inform the parents of the report. They were both extremely relieved that she had survived the crash and yet also frightened of what the final outcome may be for their beloved daughter.

We sat together for what felt like an eternity as we awaited further information. I went back to the E.R. about every twenty minutes to see if Jane had arrived back from her CAT scan but the news was slow in coming. The cries of the innocent and frightened children continued to ring throughout the ER. As I sat with this family I found out a great deal about them and their outlook on life.

This modest working class family was very rich in faith and had a positive outlook on life and love. They did not follow a religious path, but they were intensely spiritual in nature. They spoke about how fortunate they were to be able to be together and raise their children happy and healthy. They spoke about our country and how great it is. They spoke about how their parents came to America from Mexico to create a better life for their children. America had been good to them. They shared, "While we don't have a lot of money, we always have God's grace with us."

Again, I went back to the E.R. this time being informed that Jane had a serious fracture of the leg that would require surgery, and a broken arm that would need a cast. The rest of her bruises and scrapes were superficial. There was no brain damage and she would make a full recovery. I informed the family immediately and told them they could see Jane in about a half-an-hour. They were ecstatic and the tears streaming down their cheeks were now tears of gladness, gratitude and hope. I stayed with them until nightfall when Jane was eventually moved in to a room where she would remain until undergoing surgery on her leg the next morning.

I exited the E.R. I saw some of my colleagues that were also finished for the day. Amongst those they had been supporting, there were some children suffering from serious injuries and others with only minor cuts and bruises. All the children, including the bus driver, would survive. I sat with my peers and we spoke about our feelings this day. We spoke about the alarm going off in our inner being when there is distress. We also spoke about being a strong person on the outside, and how we accomplish this even when weakened on the inside. It had been quite a day for all of us. We supported each other during this crisis.

The next day I sat with the family as Jane went through her surgery. All was fine. I visited her during her rehab in the weeks that followed. During this time, I had formed a bond with little Jane. We told each other jokes and she told me about her school, her playmates, her family and her cat. When I needed to lighten up after the heaviness of my day, I would visit Jane and she always delighted me and made me laugh. When the time came for her to go home, she hugged me and said with a big smile, "Be cool, Leon."

At the time of this story, seat belts were not required on school busses. I am pleased to report that since this time, a light has been shined on this issue and many states are requiring that seat belts be installed in new school busses. However, older school busses still do not have seat belts. My prayer is that all who become aware of this glaring omission of safety regulations affecting our children, to write to their Congressional representative and lobby for change.

Partners & Lovers

I WAS CALLED UPON TO VISIT THE INTENSIVE CARE UNIT (ICU) to be with a woman whose death was imminent. I knew her story as she had been in and out of the hospital for several weeks. She would die within a matter or hours, or a few days at most.

Carol was lying in bed, as so many are when I arrive. She only weighed about 85 pounds and her huge eyes were accentuated by her small, round bald head. Her body was withered from the many cancer therapy treatments she had received. Sitting with Carol and tenderly holding her hand was a woman singing softly to her. The gentle smile on her face was overshadowed by the fear showing in her eyes. I stood in the corner of the hospital room until the singing woman addressed me. I did not want to disrupt the holy exchange of energy passing between them. The singing visitor glanced my way and explained that Carol was her soul-mate. She introduced herself as Hannah. They have been life partners, lovers, best friends and soul mates for thirty-six years. Hannah shared some of their life stories with me.

They adopted and raised two children who were now leading their own lives. She told me that their children, and grandchildren were to arrive from other states later in the day. With tears, Hannah's only wish was that Carol would live long enough to see her family arrive.

At this point, a new charge nurse who had just come on duty entered the room and asked Hannah about her relationship to the patient. Hannah replied that Carol is her soul-mate and partner. The nurse said, "You are not allowed to be here. Only family is allowed to be present in this

Intensive Care Unit. You have to leave immediately".

Hannah exclaimed, "But we are partners! We raised our children together! We've been together for thirty-six years!"

Hannah's face swelled with redness and terror and the veins in her forehead bulged with fear and adrenaline. Witnessing this, I stepped in and requested an audience with the Director of Nursing for the hospital. Sitting in her office I told her the story of what had happened at the unit. During this time, Hannah was waiting in the Visitors Lounge. After hearing this story, the Director of Nursing softly told me that she too, had a life partner. She called the ICU and instructed the staff to allow Hannah visitation rights. Relieved, Hannah went back to sit with her beloved in the ICU.

A short time later, Carol's parents, who had not ever accepted Carol and Hannah's relationship, arrived at the hospital. Carol had been estranged from her family of birth for decades because the family disapproved of her lifestyle. Carol had been harassed ever since "coming out," and was told over and over that she would "burn in hell."

Carol's mother shrieked, "Get away from my daughter! You have no right to be here." Upon hearing the commotion, staff immediately ran into the room. Carol's mother still screaming, "I am the legal next of kin," and I don't want this woman near my daughter." Although Carol was comatose, her motionless body began to tremble. It is a known fact that the sense of hearing will be the last sense to leave a patient, although they are in a comatose state. I knew from seeing Carol's body react, that she was able to hear this horrific exchange.

I escorted Hannah back to the waiting room and now Carol was alone with her parents. I sat with Hannah for several hours, holding her hand with very few spoken words. Several hours later, in the early evening, Hannah and Carol's daughter, son and grandchildren arrived. The young grandchildren waited with their grandmother, Hannah, in the visitor's lounge, as their parents went to see their other grandma, Carol.

I escorted the family into the room while Hannah remained in the lounge. Carol's parents looked at these people and said, "who are you?" Carol's son and daughter replied, "We are her children. Are you our grandparents?" Carol's mother and father, took a step back. They did not even know they were grandparents. Decades back they told Carol never to contact them as long as she was involved in this unacceptable lesbian relationship. And Carol never did ever speak to them again. I was privy to all this sad information, as Hannah shared the family story with me during our time in the Visitor's Lounge.

At this point, I interceded, and introduced myself as the Chaplain to Carol's parents. They appeared to be in shock. I asked them if they would like to talk a bit and escorted them to the "quiet room," a room set aside for reflection, physician's reports to families within the ICU unit --- space other than the Visitors Lounge.

During the time I was with Carol's parents, her son and daughter were able to be alone with their dying mother, without any distraction. In the quiet room, Carol's father did not speak. Her mother told me that Carol was their only child and knowing that she was in this relationship, they also knew they would never have the pleasure of grandchildren, like other, what they considered, "normal" families.

I spoke to them about the deep relationship that Carol and Hannah had revealed to me. After all these years, Carol's parents were finally able to comprehend the fact that loving, holy relationships can flourish, other than between a man and a woman. After speaking for about an hour, I asked them if they would like to meet their four great grandchildren, who were waiting with Hannah, their other grandmother, in the Visitor's Lounge. Again, a shocked expression was revealed on their faces, because in addition to just finding out they were grandparents, they now became great grandparents, as well. I invited them to remain in the quiet room, giving them time to process this information alone and returned to Carol's room.

Some time later, I was able to see that Carol's parents left the quiet room and were passing by her hospital room. Because I didn't know if they were leaving the hospital without any type of closure, I followed them. They went to the Visitors Lounge. They approached Hannah and asked her if they could meet her grandchildren. Hannah introduced the children and said, "These are your great grandparents, Grand-mom Carol's parents." They knelt down with tears flowing and embraced the four little ones. They composed themselves, looked to Hannah, and told her they were going in to see their daughter again. They asked Hannah to join them in Carol's room.

LGBTQIA --- Lesbian, Gay, Bi-sexual, Transgender, Questioning, Intersex and Asexual --- is not a disease or disorder. Homophobia, in all its devastating manifestations, cripples the mind and spirit. I believe that we are all searching for our soul mates during our lifetime. Carol and Hannah were blessed to find each other when they were very young, at a time in the country, when such a relationship was unacceptable by so many. Their lives were normal. They both had good, well-paying careers. They raised two healthy, well-adjusted children. They owned their own home. They tended their garden. They had a wide circle of loving friends, both straight and gay. They were active in their communities and taught their children well. In spite of all this, still, they were judged and deemed to have unacceptable lives by Carol's parents and others in our society. It is such a tragedy that Carol's parents missed so much. They tossed aside a relationship with their only child because they condemned their daughter's truths. We are judged on what we wear, the car we drive, what our home looks like, who are friends are, and our lifestyle. If our lifestyle, beliefs, religion is other than our personal belief, we tend to judge. Most religions teach us that we are made in the image of God. We are all, no matter what our sexual preferences may be, made in God's image.

Although the laws of the land are changing to protect the rights of the LGBQTIA community, allowing visitation rights, allowing marriage, allowing open military service, still people who don't agree with this, will judge. I have been taught that during our lifetime, and especially at the end of life, we have to do an accounting of our soul. This means we have to look at our actions and behavior towards others, as well as ourselves, with truth. A tale that I like to recall says that after we leave the world, we are placed in front of two screens, each telling a story. One reveals the life that we lived, and the other, the life we could have lived, if we were aligned with our truth and heart. Don't wait until you leave the world to find out which screen matched your life.

My Precious Angel

AN IMPORTANT LESSON I HAVE LEARNED as a chaplain, is that many times when our loved ones are injured, ill or in a terminal state, we as health care providers, whether doctors, social workers, nurses, social workers, etc. have to disconnect from our training and be present as a loving family member for our loved one. This is a difficult task. I have asked family members, who are also health care providers, to leave the room so I can speak with them in confidence, and tell them that their role is now changed. Their role is now that of a family member, not a health care provider. In all instances, they have thanked me for the permission to be the loved one.

The next story, which is about my youngest daughter, taught me this extremely difficult lesson. When we disengage our duties as a health care worker, and have the confidence in our peers that our loved ones will receive the physical and emotional care needed for their recovery, we then can be fully present for our family member. When my mother-in-law was in hospice care and death very close, I asked one of my colleagues to be her Chaplain in order for me to be her son.

JENNIFER, MY DAUGHTER, WAS SEVEN YEARS YOUNG. The tiny and spunky tomboy played baseball with the boy's team and was the only girl chosen for the all-star team. She would tuck her long hair under her baseball cap, and what remained were her strikingly beautiful round eyes. She liked to watch sports with me and consistently impressed me knowing all the players on the Major League teams. At home, after school and on the weekends she would play football in the middle of the street with the other neighborhood teenagers. She always had a joke to tell and witty answers for even the most benign questions and conversations. Many people of all ages gravitated to her. The best way I can describe her would be a charming and friendly little trouble-maker.

One day, many years before I even dreamed of a career in chaplaincy, while I was in my office I received a phone call from the local policy informing me that seven-year old, Jenni, was hit by a car as she was walking home from school. She was hit, run over and dragged through the street. They didn't tell me about her condition. My office was close by and I rushed to the scene as they were transferring her to an ambulance. My other daughter Amy, age eleven at the time, was walking close by and witnessed what happened. Paramedics at the scene told Amy to kneel down and shout into her sister's ear to "come back." Amy did this with love, fear and trauma. I jumped in the ambulance and drove to the hospital, holding Jenni's hand and praying. Her small body was limp and showed little life. She was unconscious, bleeding, the extent of her injuries not yet known. Six doctors and many nurses immediately tended to her in the trauma room. She had multiple external and internal injuries. She was rushed to surgery.

Bloomington, Indiana, where this occurred, is a small college town and the accident was quickly reported on the local news. As Jackie and I exited the trauma room there were about sixty people in the waiting area. We did not know these people. They heard the accident report on the radio and came to pray for our daughter. The prayer power of these strangers was holy. They came from different cultures and via various spiritual pathways. I knew they were all going to the same Source. I was overwhelmed by the love and generosity of our local townspeople.

The room in the pediatric Intensive Care Unit of the hospital was exposed, in order for the nurses to have fast access to the patients. Jackie and I entered the room after Jenni was settled from her surgery. She lay motionless in a crib. She had intravenous tubes coming from her skinny arms supporting the miraculous fight our body tends to engage in after trauma. The room was filled with monitors that displayed her heartbeat and other vital signs, connecting us in a strange way with our daughter's chances. All the rooms in the unit were the same and nurses were scurrying about from room to room. The faces of other parents told us we were not alone in our fear. We were all in the position of fear, confusion and desperately seeking solace and a hopeful promise from the eyes of any who would stop, recognize us and offer comfort.

Eventually the doctor came and shared with us the extent of her injuries. Between Jackie and I, when we finally mustered the courage to ask *the* question, namely, "...but, will she *live?*" He answered gravely serious, "her injuries are quite severe and I suggest you pray for her recovery now." He went on to say that she had suffered head trauma, and if she survives, he cannot guarantee she will recover to her former self, the rambunctious, funny and infinitely lovable daughter that remained a spark of joyful energy for so many of our family and friends.

Jenni remained in a coma for three days and, of course, we did not leave her side. Each morning I would bind my arm with *tefillin* and say the morning prayers. I would remove my *tallit*, which we also used as Jenni's personal blanket, wrapping it around her body. After praying for Jenni, I walked around the unit and stopped at the entrance of each room. There I would offer a prayer for healing to every patient on the floor. The others on the floor were also clinging to a sliver of hope. I prayed to God for their healing and survival. I also prayed, if they did not survive, God forbid, their soul would be protected and their family's hearts would remain opened to the greater meaning through such tragic ordeals. This was the week that I learned how to talk to God in the deepest way. When praying for the life of your child, the soul opens and deepens to the place beyond superficiality ---

as though the connection to the Holy One of Blessing becomes a pathway of pure light.

It was Friday at sunset, just before the beginning of *Shabbat*. My other children, Michael and Amy, came to the hospital. They brought *challah*, the *kiddish* cup and a small vile of grape juice. We went to the tiny chapel at Bloomington Hospital where we held hands, said *kiddish* and the *ha'motzi bracha* and welcomed in the *Shekhinah*, the *Sabbath* Queen, and asked for healing and a full recovery for Jenni.

When we arrived back in the ICU, we saw doctors and nurses exiting Jenni's room. Fear overtook us as we ran to the room. "Was she alive?" we thought, together, united in our concern. We surrounded her crib. The room was full with staff. She was awake! She was complaining about the heart monitor, which she had mistaken for a television monitor, and wanted the channel changed. Not knowing her mental status, difficult to discern between what she was saying and the still drugged state as she was just coming to, I leaned over the crib and trembling, I asked, "Jenni, do you know me?" She looked up and said, "you're Daddy!" My eyes overflowed with relief knowing that the severity of her brain injury was minimal. I then asked, "Do you know what happened to you?" She softly answered, "I don't know what happened, but while I was dead I met Elijah the Prophet, and I promised to share my life with him." All in the room were stunned, naturally, including us. Jenni was an innocent seven year old who could not have possibly made up such a story. I knew from her innocence and truth that she was telling her story of a near death experience. She spoke in a nonchalant tone --- simply letting us know what happened to her. She related her story in the same manner as she would tell us about an incident on the ball field --- business, as usual.

Elijah the Prophet is the prophet of healing. Jackie was later told that one of the reasons she survived was that the car in front of her at the moment of the accident was being driven by a paramedic who had just the day before been released from the Marines. He actually lifted the stopped car from her body, and kept her from going into shock. When we attempted to find this man to thank him we were unable. Did he exist? We are taught that the prophet Elijah takes on many life forms to accomplish his work. Was he there, at that crucial moment with Jenni?

Jenni spent another week in the hospital. Her recovery at home took about nine months. She impatiently fully recovered and has only a distinctive scar of remembrance on her right arm where the surgery was done. As she grew stronger, it was hard to hold her down. It was springtime and she could see her friends playing ball outside her bedroom, where she was confined. The kids would come in and visit, but she was terribly sad when they left her behind in bed. One time, she snuck out of the house, against doctors orders, tried to get into the game, and promptly fell down, cracking her front tooth --- yet another injury! Eventually, the injuries healed, the bandages came off and her spirit revived, as did ours.

The doctor had previously told us that medically, there was a small chance for her to have such a recovery, and actually the doctors on her team were amazed that she survived.

*   *   *

All through my life, I've been taught that Elijah the Prophet is the Prophet of healing. We call upon him asking for a good week at the end of *Shabbat*. We welcome him into our Passover *seder* and we even pour a glass of wine for him. Prior to Jenni's brush with death, I thought of Elijah as a great myth. How many times have we come close to an accident, or even a near death experience. We can all be Elijah the Prophet for each other. Are great healers who have changed the world for the better acting the role of Elijah? Was my wife Jackie who snatched an infant just about to crawl into a dance circle with someone who was about to stomp on the child, acting as this baby's Elijah the Prophet? Elijah takes the form of the person who is there just at the right time of need. Most people who have encountered Elijah have no idea or don't recognize what just occurred. We never met the holy Marine, Jenni's Elijah of the moment, who saved her life.

For an update, Jenni, as of the writing of this book, has a beautiful daughter named Abigail, and a young son named Elijah.

Conclusion

I HOPE THESE STORIES YOU HAVE NOW READ opened space in your heart, enabling them to penetrate more fully as lessons for your own life. We all have stories that awaken our awareness, arousing and opening greater vistas, which allow us to grow more fully, even prior to actually undergoing such experiences. My wish for you is that you may deeply embrace these stories to further aid in your fundamental understanding that is already within you and to comprehend that our life's journey is short and fragile Our job is to measure and treasure each moment --- good moments and those not so good. Know that each moment of our lives will not last --- each moment will pass into eternity. When I review my life's journey, I come to see that nothing ever stays the same --- everything is always changing.

As we walk this tight rope of life, the same fine line mentioned in the introduction of this book, where it is so uncertain as to whether we can keep our balance, our center, we must grasp the fact that our lives do not follow a straight path; it consists of constant curves and detours. When we are in our cars and come upon a detour we become irritated because we know we will lose time and may have to go to unfamiliar places. My wish is that the unfamiliar spaces you have encountered in the stories will not upset you, but allow you to see that the detour and bumps in the road of your life as a blessing, a learning tool and an opportunity for expansion. When I encountered the holy beggar who offered a deep blessing to both my family, and me I was feeling annoyed because, just prior, I had come across a literal detour in the road and I was taken off my usual path. If it weren't for the detour, I would not have met the holy beggar and not received his blessing. Know that if you allow these detours, these hills and valleys to take you to a destination of understanding and acceptance, to a broader perspective, where you will receive guidance and clarity, then each day, each moment becomes a journey of joyful curiosity, wonder and love.

Perhaps if we really hear the higher power's message of love, we can truly fulfill the commandment to "Love the other as oneself." When you choose to strip away the layers in your heart that have enveloped your soul with grief, anger or dismay, your healing process can begin.

We are on the tightrope of feelings, shattered dreams and fear. We know that balancing on the tight rope we call life, brings moments of stumbling, moments of having to dust off the pain, anger, feelings of failure and loss, and then having the courage and faith to continue on life's journey. We are hungry, but not for food. We are restless, but not for exercise. We are thirsty, but not for water. I challenge, encourage and bless you to walk on the tight rope of life, sating your hunger and thirst *and* your restlessness with the love that is inherent in your own heart. When we open ourselves to the larger world, the larger perspective, what may seem strange to us becomes the familiar and may even become divine. If we allow constriction to overtake our bodies and minds, we are pilfering from God's gift of expansive possibilities.

Pastoral care and caring arises from many pathways. I hope that you've learned that if we see a person in need, we are obligated to react. We never know when we can change a person's life, deepen their connection to the sacred, fill them with some hope and, while on this path, our lives become enriched and expanded as well.

Glossary of Hebrew and Yiddish Words

Ani – I

Avotaynu – Our fathers

Ayin – The 18th letter of the Hebrew Alphabet

Ba'al HaBracha – Master of the Holy Blessing

Beshert – Meant to be

Bedeken – Part of the Jewish wedding ceremony where the groom puts the veil on the bride

Bubbie – Grandmother

Chai – Life

Challah – Ceremonial bread

Chassidic – Branch of Orthodox Judaism that promotes spirituality through Jewish mysticism; also Hasidic

Chatan – Groom

Chazzan – Cantor, prayer leader of song

Chochma – Wisdom

Chuppahh – Jewish wedding canopy

D'var – Teaching on a torah portion

Echad – One

El Molay Rachamim – "God full of compassion," Prayer recited at a funeral

Emotaynu – Our mothers

Etz Chaim – Tree of life, the wooden poles that the Torah is attached to

Havdalah – Ceremony marking the end of the Sabbath

Kabbalah – Jewish Mystical Text(s)

Kaddish – Prayer said in memory of the dead

Kaddosh – Holy, first words of a prayer

Kallah – Bride

Ketubah – Wedding contract

Kishkes – Guts

Klipa – Shell

L'dor v' dor – From generation to generation

Mazel – Luck

Melech – King

Mem – Middle letter of the Hebrew alphabet

Mensch – An honorable person who does the right thing

Midrash – Stories interpreting torah verses

Mikveh – A ritual bath

Mi sheberach – Prayer for healing

Mishnah – First collection of Oral Torah redacted by Rabbi Yehuda Ha
    Nasi in 220 CE

Mitzrayim – Egypt, the narrowed places

Modeh – Thanks, grateful

Neshama – Soul

Niggun – Jewish religious melody usually without words

Parsha Schlach – Torah portion in Numbers

Pesach – Passover

Pirke Avot – Ethics of the Fathers, a tractate (chapter) of the Mishnah

Psalms – Songs, praises a book of the Bible

Rabbi – Teacher of Torah

Reb – Honorific title denoting teacher

Reb Nachman of Bratslav – Founder of Chassidism

Rebbe – Yiddish for Rabbi

Rebbono Shel Olam – Master of the Universe

Refuah shlema and refuah ha guf – A healing of body, mind, and spirit.

Schmooze – To talk intimately or informally

Sefer – Book

Shaliach tzibor – Messenger of the congregation, one who leads prayer

Shalom – Peace, wholeness

Shechinah – Female indwelling presence of God

Shema – Listen, the central prayer in Judaism

Sheva Brachot – Seven blessings said at a wedding

Shin – Second to last letter of Hebrew alphabet

Shiva – Mourning period after death

Shofrot – Ram's horns (singular Shofar) sounded on the Jewish High
    Holidays to remind people to listen

Shul – Synagogue

Sinai – Mount Sinai where Moses received the Ten Commandments

Smicha – Ordination of a rabbi within Judaism

Tallit – Prayer shawl

Talmud – Rabbinic law and literature expounding on the Torah

T'kiyah Shevarim T'ruah T'kiyah – Sounds of the shofar, transliterated as:
    T'kiyah Shevarim T'kiyah
    T'kiyah T'ruahT'kiyah
    T'kiyah Gadola

Teshuva – Return, repentence

Torah – Instruction, teaching the five books of Moses and can also mean
    all oral and written Rabbinic commentaries

Tuchas – Derriere

Vidui – Confessional prayer, end of life atonement

Yaacov – Jacob

Yamode – "Come up," first words of being called to the Torah

"Yis-gad-dal v'yis-kad-dash sh'mey rab-bo…" – first words of the Kaddish,
    the mourner's prayer

z'l – Abbreviation for *zichrono l'vracha*, "may his memory be for a blessing," said in memory of a deceased person